Museum of London

Museum of London

Valerie Cumming • Nick Merriman • Catherine Ross

First published in 1996 by
Scala Publishers Ltd
Gloucester Mansions
140a Shaftesbury Avenue
London WC2H 8HD

Reprinted 1999, 2002

ISBN 1 85759 127 5

Edited, designed and typeset by
Book Creation Services Ltd, London
Printed and bound by Editoriale Lloyd
Trieste, Italy

Acknowledgements
Within the Museum of London a great many colleagues have
assisted with the preparation of this book. The editors are grateful
to John Clark, Jonathan Cotton, Hazel Forsyth, Jenny Hall,
Cheryl Thorogood and Rosemary Weinstein in the Early
Department, and to Edwina Ehrman, Wendy Evans, Mireille
Galinou, Rory O'Connell, Javier Pes, Mike Seaborne and Alex
Werner in the Later Department. The Conservation Department
all spent time preparing material for the photography which was
taken by Torla Evans, John Chase and Richard Stroud. Many
thanks to all of them and to Gavin Morgan in Photographic
Records and to Suzie Burt, Publications Officer. Especial thanks
go to Chris Ellmers who contributed the section on Port and
River History Collections. This was a team effort by everyone
concerned: those named above and others who took an interest
in, encouraged and supported the project throughout.

Contents

Foreword

The Museum of London exists to inspire a passion for London. As the single most important source of knowledge on the nation's capital, it is uniquely both a national and local museum. This book provides just a glimpse of the extraordinary breadth of the Museum's rare collections. Over a million objects are held in the Museum's stores, cared for by curators and conservators who are all leaders in their field. The permanent galleries, together with imaginative temporary exhibitions, tell the city's story from prehistoric times to today – collecting, investigating and displaying every aspect of London life.

The Museum also holds the largest archaeological archive in Europe and has a vital role to play as mediator and interpreter of this wealth of information. Archaeological discoveries are used by the Museum to communicate information simply and instil a sense of ownership of the past.

The Museum of London is committed to recording and explaining change in every part of London life. It continues to reflect the extraordinary story of this vibrant world city. It continues to be London's memory.

Dr Simon Thurley, *Director*

The Development of the Collections

'Antiquities are history defaced, or some remnants of history which have escaped the shipwreck of time.'
Francis Bacon

Fire of London model, 1914
This model, still on display in the Museum of London in a modified form, was made by the firm of J.B.Thorp and paid for by J.G.Joicey.

THE MUSEUM OF LONDON is a unique institution. Its antecedents, constitution and range of collections set it apart from the generality of museums in the United Kingdom. Its complicated history is very well recorded in Francis Sheppard's *The Treasury of London's Past* (HMSO, 1990). In this brief introduction, only the slightest skeleton of this story will be sketched in order to illuminate the development of the collections. Those seeking the lively but often strange occurrences that surround the entire history are recommended to read Dr Sheppard's book.

The Museum of London of the 1990s exists to record and represent the history of a major international city in all of its diversity. It traces London's history from the earliest prehistoric settlements in the region up to the present day. A museum that first opened its doors to the public in December 1976 should, in theory, have a tightly structured collection and only a modest history. The structure, however, exists as a relatively recent policy unifying collections drawn from two much older and separate institutions. Much of what is displayed by the Museum in its permanent galleries and in temporary exhibitions is drawn from the collections formed by the Guildhall Museum and the London Museum. There have, naturally, been significant changes of emphasis in recent years. One major change is that curators are now highly selective and consider their collecting activities carefully. What the Museum needs in order to fulfil its purposes, why it needs certain types of artefact, and how it will use and care for any new acquisitions, informs all collecting initiatives.

The elder of the two parents of the Museum of London was the Guildhall Museum, founded by the Corporation of London in 1826 and administered by the Corporation's Librarian. Its remit was to provide 'a suitable place for the reception of such Antiquities as relate to the City of London, and Suburbs, as may be procured, or presented to the Corporation'. It was a significant initiative at a time when a process of development within London was revealing antiquities of the Roman and medieval periods with increasing regularity.

In the 1820s and 1830s the study and collection of British antiquities was mostly an amateur, gentlemanly pastime, with individual collectors forging relationships with workmen involved with the many improvement schemes. Workmen sold finds to interested collectors for ready cash, and there was little systematic recording of find spots or context for these artefacts.

From the 1840s onwards considerable amounts of excavated material found their way into the Museum, such as the antiquities found at the Royal Exchange site in 1841. The range of the collections extended to include tradesmen's tokens (the H.B. Hanbury Beaufoy collection), badges, medals of City guilds, inn and shop signs, and church plate. These were

Material found at the National Safe Deposit Company site (*below*)
These Roman antiquities, found during building works near the Mansion House, were presented to the Guildhall Museum in 1875.

'Daily Life in London' (*right*)
This case from 1912 gives an impression of the density of the displays at Kensington Palace.

not acquired in a particularly systematic manner, and antiquities from the earlier periods of London's history remained the Guildhall Museum's speciality.

Gradually the Corporation of London got into the habit of purchasing new acquisitions: for example, £200 was spent on Thomas Gunston's collection of Roman and medieval antiquities in the 1850s. Then in the early 1870s the construction of a new library and museum prompted the Corporation to vote £500 'for the purchase of such objects of antiquarian interest as may be considered desirable for furnishing the Museum recently erected'. The practice, not unusual at the time, was to acquire complete or part collections formed by enthusiastic and knowledgeable amateurs. To this day it is possible to identify material from the National Safe Deposit Company, from John Walker Baily, James Smith and the Rev. S.M. Mayhew's collections, all of which were donated or purchased in the 1870s and 1880s.

By the late 1880s the collection was substantial, and thoughts turned to the production of a catalogue. This endeavour took fifteen years and produced a sturdy volume, with photographs which provided useful visual amplification of the printed descriptions. The range of the collections listed was impressive, but their strength was still in the early periods of London's history. This emphasis continued to be at the forefront of all subsequent collecting initiatives. In 1907, a mere eighty-one years after the Museum was founded, a dedicated member of staff was appointed to care for its interests. The 'museum clerk', Frank Lambert, was soon enthusiastically engaged in all aspects of museum activity, one of his key duties being 'to watch all

excavations within the City'; he also introduced a
number of modern techniques into the Museum. After a
quiet period in the 1920s and 1930s, the Museum was
moved to the Royal Exchange after the war, due to
bomb damage at Guildhall, and then to its final home,
Gillett House. Its premises were too cramped to do
justice to the collections, especially so when it received
important additions from sites such as the Temple of
Mithras and other parts of the city undergoing
redevelopment after the ravages of wartime.

Close involvement in the development of
archaeological investigation in the City of London
remained a significant feature of the Museum's existence.
A department of urban archaeology was set up in 1973 to
ensure that key sites were excavated and that the
archaeological process was closely allied to the Museum
rather than separately organised by universities and local
societies. Thus, collections were acquired site by site
rather than in a piecemeal fashion, and complete
assemblages of material replaced individual artefacts as the
most informative record of the early periods of London's
history.

Unlike the Guildhall Museum, the London Museum
did not move slowly into the business of forming a
collection. Without a building or a significant group of exhibits but with the
promise of funds from an anonymous benefactor in search of a title, its three
trustees, Lords Beauchamp and Esher and the Hon. Lewis Harcourt, wrote
to *The Times* appealing for support in March 1911. Although when the
Museum opened to the public a year later the *Museums Journal* reviewer
could not identify 'the guiding principle on which the collection had been
assembled', the basic rationale was that given in *Twenty-Five Years of the
London Museum* (1937). This stated that the 'main purpose of the Museum
was to illustrate the daily life and history of London in all ages' – an apparent
duplication of the Guildhall Museum's role. This was easily overlooked by
the trustees of the London Museum and by its dynamic keeper, Guy Laking.
He quickly forged a productive relationship with the dealer in antiquities
G. F. Lawrence over much-needed acquisitions. The first recorded purchase
from Lawrence was on 4 April 1911, less than a month after the idea of the
Museum had been mooted in public. This was an interesting axis, for
Lawrence had previously sold antiquities to the Guildhall Museum and also,
between 1901 and 1904, had been employed to work on that museum's
catalogue. So, from the outset there was a conflict of interest between the
two museums, one located in the heart of the historic Roman and medieval
city, the other in a royal palace in Kensington.

Socially, if not intellectually, the London Museum was in a different class
to the Guildhall Museum. The triumvirate of trustees had the ear and the
patronage of the Royal Family and the government, and, in Guy Laking, a
keeper who could charm potential benefactors with a combination of
lightly-worn scholarship and a very real flair for press and public relations.
It was an unbeatable combination, and by the time the Museum opened to
the public in April 1912 it had acquired a collection of over 18,000 artefacts,
many of which had been written up and illustrated in the newspapers, as had

the private visit by King George V and Queen Mary on 21 March. On its opening day there were long queues waiting to see this highly publicised new museum.

The swiftly acquired collection which so confused the *Museums Journal* reviewer comprised a combination of loans, donations and purchases. Many Londoners were stimulated by the advance publicity into offering material, and their cherished possessions were displayed alongside groups carefully assembled by skilful collectors from whom collections had been bought or borrowed. Naturally, to open a fully fledged museum only twelve months after announcing its launch implied that certain collections had been intended as a nucleus. One such was the Hilton Price collection of antiquities and bygones. This included a wide range of excavated material, from prehistory to the early modern period, and assorted tools, implements, toys, leather items and similar categories of later date. The early accession registers are thin on detail, but 'A1568 Milk tooth of Mammoth found in Pall Mall' is a resonant example. This collection had been bought by Lewis Harcourt for £2000 in October 1910, well in advance of the public announcement of the Museum into which it was to be placed. Complete or partial collections were the backbone of the new displays, with costume bought from the history painter J.A. Seymour Lucas, royal costume and toys lent by Queen Mary, and London antiquities loaned and then given by Dr

Frank Corner. Donations were also made by the Chairman of Trustees, Lewis Harcourt, his earliest recorded gift being a 'Washing bowl from the Condemned cell, Newgate Prison', and by the keeper, Guy Laking, an arms and armour specialist, whose gifts included 'thumbscrews' and 'handcrushers'. In 1912 a substantial gift from Jonathan King of forty large scrapbooks – containing toy theatres, valentines, Christmas cards and over a hundred tinsel pictures – laid the foundation for an important collection of printed ephemera. Purchases were made of costume and textile items, prints, drawings and oil paintings. Drawings of the earliest periods in London's history and five models were commissioned. Many of these elements, which proved such popular exhibits in displays at Kensington Palace and Lancaster House, still fascinate visitors to the Museum of London today.

It is impossible to provide case studies of each of the major benefactors, but a handful will illustrate the generosity and commitment shown to the London Museum from its inception. One of the most notable of the early benefactors was John G. Joicey. After reading the letter to *The Times* in March 1911, he offered to lend items of Chelsea and Bow porcelain and some 'Battersea' enamels from his personal

collection. The Laking charm worked its usual
wonders, and shortly after the two men met the
embryonic museum received substantial
groups of all three types of material. Towards
the end of December 1911 a group of
important watches by London makers
also arrived. All of these items were
converted from loans to gifts on 20
March 1912, the day before the private
royal visit to the new museum. The
china included candlesticks, cups,
dishes, figures, jugs, plates and vases; the
enamels were in the form of boxes, étuis,
needlecases, scent flacons and trays.
Despite later reattributions of some of this
material, this was benefaction on the grand scale;
and it continued with more loans, which included snuff boxes,
silverware, jewellery, clocks, pistols, costume, embroidery, prints, a sedan
chair, and a specimen of early printing that was thought to be by William
Caxton. Of this generous but wholly undemanding man, Laking wrote
'unlike most donors of Collections he expects nothing in return'. However,
Queen Mary's Privy Chamber at Kensington Palace was renamed 'The
Joicey Room' in his honour, coinciding with his presentation of all of the
additional loans as a gift to the Museum on 7 March 1913. This reclusive
man continued his support in subsequent years. When the Museum moved
into its new premises at Lancaster House, Joicey sent, from Florence, early in
1914 three large chests of 'English' costume dating from the late sixteenth to
the late eighteenth centuries. He also ordered and paid for models for the
new displays, including ones of the Great Fire of London and a Frost Fair on
the Thames, which were installed in the autumn of 1914 . Joicey died in July
1919, three months before the Museum was due to reopen in October, after
wartime closure, and shortly before Guy Laking's early death in November
1919. Laking's legacy was a dynamic and popular museum, like no other.

Joicey's collections enriched the eclectic but
chronological approach to London's history
pioneered by Laking; in addition, through
the terms of his will, he continued his
benefaction beyond the grave, with the J.G.
Joicey Fund to assist with purchases for the
collections.

Other early collections associated with
the names of their donors are the Tangye
and Garton collections. Sir Richard Tangye
had assembled around a thousand items
which related to the Civil War period and,
most especially, to Oliver Cromwell. It
contained books, manuscripts, paintings,
miniatures, seals, medals, coins and small
items of memorabilia. It was acquired
through the good offices of Lewis Harcourt
in June 1912, but not mentioned as a gift or
displayed until after the Museum had

Group of penny toys
Some of the thousand penny toys given to the London Museum by Ernest King in 1918. King acquired most of his toys from the street peddlers who traditionally sold their wares just before Christmas on Ludgate Hill.

Wine glass
Wine glass with the arms of Sir Robert Ladbroke, Lord Mayor of London in 1747, who was renowned for his entertaining. This glass may have been made at the Whitefriars glasshouse. It comes from the Garton collection of glass, which came to the Museum in 1934.

Musical clock, c. 1760
George Pyke (active from 1753)
This virtuoso piece of London clockmaking was given to the London Museum in 1913 by J.G. Joicey. At four-hourly intervals the clock plays a tune and figures in the painted landscape move.

moved and reopened at Lancaster House in March 1914. It was given by Sir Richard's son, Harold, who on 14 June 1912 became a baronet in the king's Birthday Honours list. Cause and effect? Almost certainly so. No such reward was bestowed on the heirs of Sir Richard Garton when they converted a loan, made at Garton's death in 1934, to a gift in 1943. Comprising 437 pieces, this is one of the finest privately assembled collections of English glass. It ranges in date from mid-seventeenth-century pieces to early-nineteenth-century ones. The goblets and wine glasses are particularly fine, but there are also other types of glass, such as bowls, candlesticks and decanters. Despite the size of the collection few pieces are identical, and among its strengths are important commemorative glass vessels from the eighteenth century.

By the time the twenty-fifth anniversary book was published the list of benefactors was substantial, ranging from individuals such as Lord Duveen, J. Pierpoint Morgan, P.A.S. Phillips and Mr and Mrs Ernest Makower to major institutions like HM Office of Works, the London County Council, the Port of London Authority and the National Art Collections Fund.

At Lancaster House the arrangement of the collections on three floors and in a basement area cleverly interwove chronological galleries with equally popular displays devoted to the many strengths of the collections, including metalwork, costume, the theatre, models, architectural features (including prison cells) and transport, which encompassed the Roman boat and the Duke of Wellington's coach. These displays, spread over 60,000 square feet (about 6000 square metres) of exhibition space, were immensely popular with visitors and equally so with donors; each area was tightly packed with exhibits, but significant new acquisitions usually found their way into the appropriate display. Many important purchases were made in the 1920s and 1930s, often only possible thanks to the Museum's carefully cultivated band of benefactors. Such material included Palaeolithic implements (the Garraway Rice collection), watercolours, state crowns, costume and jewellery.

After the Second World War the government, which under the terms of the original lease had always been able to use Lancaster House for hospitality purposes, decided that it wished to be the sole occupant. From the luxury of 60,000 square feet (6000 square metres) of display space the London Museum was reduced to 15,000 square feet (about 1500 square metres)

when it reopened back at Kensington Palace in July 1951. This was seen as an interim move (it actually lasted for twenty-five years), but the Museum has never regained the amount of display space it had in its heyday in the 1920s and 1930s. However, the commitment, knowledge and enthusiasm of the small staff ensured that collections were added to, catalogues published, and temporary exhibitions created and changed, in order that visitors should enjoy a varied and informative microcosm of London's complex history. Purchases were assisted by another legacy named after its late benefactor, Dr Mackenzie Bell. A capital sum of £38,000 was invested and, like the Joicey Fund, was used primarily for acquisition purposes.

These developments took place against a background of radically changing circumstances that concerned the future of both the London Museum and the Guildhall Museum. After prolonged discussions and negotiations it was decided that they should merge, be housed in a new building in the City, and be funded in equal thirds by the government, the Corporation of London and the Greater London Council (later, after the abolition of the GLC in 1986, in equal halves by the government and the Corporation). The Museum of London Act of 1965 provided the legislative framework for the change; building work started on the new site in 1971; and the galleries opened to the public in December 1976. In advance of this there had been a flurry of collecting, especially of twentieth-century material, needed to illustrate such themes as popular publishing, the Americanisation of shopping (department stores, Woolworths interiors), the media (radio, TV and cinema), and the change from traditional crafts and industries to a service-based economy that had taken place in offices, banks and commercial firms.

Since 1976 the Museum of London has used its permanent galleries and temporary exhibition spaces extensively. More than a hundred exhibitions of every size and countless small changes of display have been presented to the public. A number reflected changes in the areas of collecting or reinterpreted long-held collections. Historic and contemporary photography, cultural diversity, archaeological discoveries and women's suffrage all represent new or revitalised strands in collecting. Other themes as diverse as London gardens, jewellery and contemporary artists' impressions of the city have added material to the existing collections. Perhaps the two areas in which the collections have grown fastest are those concerned with archaeological investigation in London, both through excavation and through the process of industrial archaeology. The archaeological archive of excavated material is now very large and comprises assemblages and paper records of hundreds of sites excavated over a period of more than twenty-five years. This is an important research resource for the early periods of London's history, but it is not

Porcelain figures, c. 1760

Bow

These figures of General Wolfe and the Marquis of Granby, made at Bow in East London, were given to the Museum by J.G. Joicey and are typical of his taste for 18th-century decorative items.

Britannia visits the London Museum, 1928

Designed by Rex Whistler (1905–44)

usually as easy to display as, for example, finds from the Thames foreshore – another significant source for small items of jewellery, toys, badges and so forth. The collections of industrial archaeology contain major groups of material which record craft skills, light-industrial processes and the impact made on London by the port and docks. They are of excellent display quality and will, it is hoped, find a home in an independent museum in Docklands. Some indication of the importance and diversity of this group of material is indicated by selected paintings and artefacts within this book, but the richness and breadth of the collections merit a separate guide to accompany the new museum.

Collecting never stops if a museum is to remain alive, but attitudes towards it have changed significantly in the most recent period of the Museum's history. Despite the exceptions mentioned above, curators are now trained to be innately selective in their proposals for new acquisitions. Every new addition to the collection has to earn its keep by demonstrating both display and research potential, and it also requires a context and supporting data. Views on what it is useful to collect have also kept pace with technological innovation, and photographs, oral history recordings, videotapes and films enter the collection both in their own right and also to provide valuable contextual information about London as a place and about its inhabitants and their views. Public awareness of the extent of museum collections has also changed in recent years, and the Museum of London is delighted to have been in the forefront of new approaches to handling sessions and access to stored collections for groups of visitors. This modern attitude ensures that the 'antiquities' of the future will not be 'history defaced' but history clarified.

London Chronology
475,000 BC — AD 2000

475,000 BC	Britain's first people arrive from the continent of Europe.
8300–1500 BC	As the climate improves, hunter-gatherers settle down to farm.
1500–500 BC	The importance of the River Thames makes the London area a focus for metalworking communities.
55 and 54 BC	Julius Caesar invades south-east Britain but later withdraws.
AD 50	Foundation of Londinium, the first London.
60	London is destroyed during a revolt by the warrior queen Boudica.
100	A rebuilt London is the largest city in Britain and capital of the Roman province.
c. 220	A massive protective wall is built around London.
350 onwards	Attacks by German tribes intensify as Roman rule weakens throughout the empire.
400–600	Angles and Saxons arrive from Germany to settle and farm the area around London.
450	By now the walled city is abandoned.
600–900	A thriving new London is established to the west of the old city, but falls prey to Viking raiders.
886 onwards	King Alfred begins to rebuild London inside the old Roman walls.
c. 1050	King Edward the Confessor builds a palace at Westminster and founds an abbey nearby.
1066	The Norman conquest brings an influx of French rulers and changes to the way in which London is governed.
c. 1078	Work starts on the building of the Tower of London.
c. 1189	The first Mayor of London takes office.
1348–9	The Black Death (bubonic plague) kills thousands of Londoners.
1387–1400	Geoffrey Chaucer writes *The Canterbury Tales*.
1476	William Caxton sets up the first printing press in England, at Westminster.
1485	Henry VII seizes power and establishes the Tudor royal line.
1534 onwards	The Reformation brings religious change. Henry VIII abolishes the monasteries and changes the face of London forever.
1558	The first map of London is published.
c. 1586	William Shakespeare arrives in London and develops a career as an actor and playwright in the theatres on the south bank of the Thames.
1598	The first guide book to London is published.
c. 1600	London is trading with America and the Far East.
1605	Guy Fawkes attempts to blow up Parliament.
1635	Inigo Jones designs the Piazza, Covent Garden.
1642–9	Civil War rages throughout the country, and Europe is shocked when King Charles I is executed in front of a public crowd in London.
1660	Samuel Pepys starts writing his diary.
1665	One in four Londoners die from the Plague.
1666	The Great Fire destroys four-fifths of the City's buildings.

1666–7 onwards	Sir Christopher Wren plans and supervises new buildings in brick and stone.
1660–9	Tea, coffee and luxury imports from China and Turkey first go on sale in London.
1675	The Royal Observatory is built at Greenwich, to the south-east of London.
1685	Protestant refugees from France settle in London in large numbers, bringing new skills.
1694	The Bank of England is founded in the City.
1711	St Paul's Cathedral is completed.
1720	Investors lose fortunes in the first investment scandal, the 'South Sea Bubble'.
1739	John Wesley, the founder of the Methodist movement, becomes an evangelist to the poor.
1750	Westminster Bridge is completed.
1755	Dr Samuel Johnson publishes his dictionary.
1787	The first convict ships from London set sail for Australia.
1802	The West India Dock opens.
1829	The Metropolitan Police Force is formed.
1831	New London Bridge opens.
1837	The new Palace of Westminster is begun.
1851	The Great Exhibition is held in Hyde Park.
1855	Metropolitan Board of Works established to improve London's infrastructure.
1863	The world's first underground railway opens.
1871	The Royal Albert Hall opens.
1887	Sir Arthur Conan Doyle creates the great fictional detective Sherlock Holmes.
1888	Londoners elect their first city-wide authority, the London County Council.
1894	Tower Bridge is completed.
1904	The first double-decker motor bus is seen on the London streets.
1908	A giant rally in Hyde Park publicises the Suffragettes' campaign for votes for women.
1909	The Port of London Authority takes control of London's vast network of docks.
1915	The first German air raid over London takes place.
1922	The BBC begins radio broadcasting.
1926	The General Strike disrupts London.
1936	The BBC introduces a regular television service.
1940	The London Blitz causes damage to buildings and severe loss of life throughout the capital.
1946	Heathrow Airport opens in west London.
1965	The first Caribbean carnival is held in Notting Hill.
1966	London County Council replaced by an extended authority, the Greater London Council.
1986	London loses its city-wide authority when the Greater London Council is abolished.
1990s	London is home to 6.9 million people, speaking 200 languages, who work in 200,000 businesses.

Prehistoric
London

Celtic coin, c. 60 BC
A gold coin ('stater') of French type with
a design showing a stylised horse and
charioteer, from Mitcham Common.

Flint hand axe, c. 350,000–120,000 BC
(*far left*)
Thousands of these all-purpose cutting and chopping tools have been found in the gravels underlying modern London. From the site of the Regent Palace Hotel, Glasshouse Street, Piccadilly.

Mesolithic tools (*left*)
A selection of flint and antler tools dating from between 8500 and 4500 BC, comprising a flint adze from the Thames at Cross Deep, Twickenham, mounted in a modern wooden sleeve; a flint arrow tip and barb from Barnes Common, set in a modern wooden shaft; and a barbed antler point from the Thames at Wandsworth.

Ground and polished axe,
c. 3900–2500 BC (*middle left*)
This axe, from the Thames at Mortlake, is unusual because it is made of jadeite. Jadeite only occurs in the western Alps, and was perhaps the ultimate status symbol in a pre-metal age.

Flint, bone and copper knives,
c. 2200–1500 BC (*below left*)
When copper was introduced it was an extremely rare new substance and a symbol of wealth. The flint and bone examples emulate the form of a copper knife in commoner materials. They were all found in the Thames in west London and are shown together with a modern reconstruction (on the left of the group).

Diorama of wild cow burial, c. 1800 BC
(*right*)
The dismembered remains of a wild cow (or aurochs) being buried in a deep pit at Harmondsworth, north of Heathrow. When the site was excavated, four flint arrowheads were found resting among the bones, showing that the animal had been hunted and deliberately buried, with only the horns removed.

A cascade of bronze weaponry, c. 1300–650 BC (*opposite*)
All of these weapons, which include rapiers, spearheads and swords, were dredged from the Thames. They may have accompanied the mortal remains of their owners into the river as part of funerary rites.

Cremation vessels, c. 1900–1400 BC (*left*)
Two pottery vessels with heavy 'collared' rims from Ham Common. Vessels of this type were often used to hold the ashes of the dead.

Horse gear, 2nd to 1st century BC (*below*)
Equipment including a three-link snaffle bit from Walthamstow, a 'terret ring' (rein guide) from the Thames at Isleworth, and a 'horn cap' from Brentford. This last piece may have been a chariot or harness fitting and is decorated with an intricate design in the Celtic style.

Roman London

**Amber and emerald necklaces,
1st to 2nd century AD**
Amber beads threaded on their original
string, and a necklace fragment of
hexagonal emerald beads with gold-wire
links. The materials used for both these
necklaces were imported into Roman
Britain. Amber came to Britain from the
Baltic, and in the Roman period emeralds
originated in Egypt. Found in Old Jewry
and Cannon Street respectively.

Mother-goddess carving, 3rd century AD (*left*)

Sculpture found re-used as building material in the late-Roman riverside wall at Blackfriars. Carved from limestone, the relief depicts four female figures seated on a bench, holding (*from right to left*) bread and fruit, a dog, a suckling baby, and a basket of fruit. They probably portray the three native mother goddesses, although the fourth figure cannot be identified.

Samian pottery, 2nd century AD (*below left*)

The Museum of London has one of the richest collections in Britain of this high-quality tableware. This group was found in an unused state during excavations at New Fresh Wharf, Lower Thames Street. It probably represents shipments of pottery broken in transit and dumped from the warehouses along the Roman waterfront. Samian was produced in France and extensively shipped to Roman Britain.

'Face pot', 1st to 3rd century AD (*right*)

Ceramic vessel, possibly from Cannon Street, with a representation of a human face. Pots of this type are found in cemeteries and in areas of religious importance, such as the Walbrook stream. It is thought that they may have been votive offerings providing general protection to the individuals who used them. It is not known what the faces are meant to portray – perhaps a human being, a god or a theatrical mask.

Military dagger and sheath, late 2nd to 3rd century AD (*below right*)

Iron dagger with a broad blade, complete with dome-pommelled handle. The sheath that held the dagger is complete except for a leather cover. Daggers were used by both the Roman legionary and auxiliary troops. From Copthall Court, City of London.

**Roman wall painting,
mid 2nd century AD**

Elaborate architectural scheme depicting
a cupid standing within a stepped
entrance-way of columns festooned
with flowered garlands. The painting is
semicircular, to fit into the curved ceiling
of a bath-house. It has a rich colour
scheme with ground colours of yellow
and expensive cinnabar red. The plaster
fell face down and lay undisturbed in a
medieval garden until it was excavated
in 1983. From the site of Winchester
Palace, Southwark.

Oculist's stamp, Roman

Stone block, belonging to Gaius Silvius Tetricus, an eye doctor (oculist). He probably came from France. His name and four different medical preparations for the relief of eye troubles are recorded around the four sides. The lettering is written in reverse, as the stone was probably used to stamp sticks of ointment. From Upper Thames Street.

Cremation group, late 1st to early 2nd century AD

Glass cinerary urn containing cremated bones, accompanied by gravegoods consisting of a square glass bottle and a glass flask. It was customary to bury the dead with enough food and drink for their journey to the Underworld. From the Roman cemetery in the northern part of the town, at Bishopsgate.

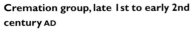

Comb and manicure set, Roman

Composite bone comb with patterned central bar. It has a choice of wide and fine teeth. The manicure set consists of five implements for personal hygiene. They include tweezers for removing unwanted hair, nail-cleaners, a nail-file and a scoop for using cosmetics. Traces of red enamel decoration remain on the bar. The set would have been suspended from a belt. From Pudding Lane and London Wall.

Belt set, late 4th to early 5th century AD

Germanic-style belt set decorated with spiral motifs and animal heads. Belts such as these were worn as badges of high rank in the civil service or army. The style of the belt indicates that the wearer was probably a German official employed as an administrator in the late Roman Empire. From a burial in the eastern cemetery at Mansell Street.

Sculptures from the Temple of Mithras

One of the major excavations of the post-war period was conducted in 1954 on the site of the Temple of Mithras at Bucklersbury House, Walbrook, by Professor W. F. Grimes, Director of the London Museum. Among the finds were these two fine sculptures, both made of marble from Carrara, Italy. The one on the left, dating from *c.* AD 180–220, depicts Mithras as a handsome youth, wearing his usual Phrygian cap. His eyes are turned away from the deed of slaying the bull, from whose blood flowed eternal life. The head probably formed part of a lifesize bull-slaying scene that would have stood in the apsidal end of the temple. The other (*right*), dating from the 2nd century AD, shows Mercury, who escorted the dead from Earth to Paradise. He is seated on a rock holding a money bag, his symbol as patron of commerce, and is accompanied by a ram and a tortoise. The ram is the symbol of fertility; the tortoises, whose shells were used to make lyres, may illustrate the eternal happiness of the afterlife as promised by Mithraism.

Mosaic and room, mid- to late 3rd century AD

Mosaic made of variously coloured cubes (*tesserae*) of stone and ceramic. Found in Queen Victoria Street, Bucklersbury, in 1869, it was revealed to the public for three days, when about 50,000 people came to view it. The reconstructed setting is of similar date, and the wall painting is based on plaster fragments from Austin Friars. The furniture consists of replicas, but all the artefacts come from Roman London.

Port model, c. AD 100

Based upon information obtained from archaeological excavations along Lower Thames Street, the model illustrates the development of Roman London's port facilities. A new quay is being built into the river, replacing an earlier timber-faced quay. Cargoes are being unloaded and stored in the warehouses that run along the waterfront. Shops, workshops and inns serve both the waterfront district and the rest of the city. A timber bridge connects the north and south settlements.

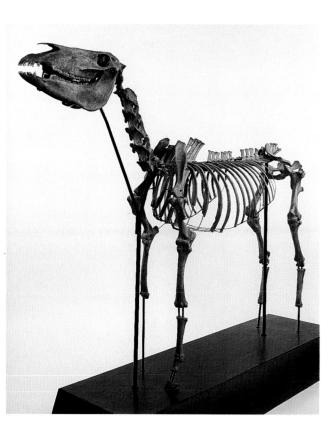

Horse skeleton, 2nd century AD

On loan from the Natural History Museum
Articulated bones of a near-complete horse, about 12 to 13 hands high. Its lumbar vertebrae are fused together, indicating that it carried heavy weights. It may have been used as a pack animal or for riding in Roman London. From Miles Lane.

Foot lamp, mid-2nd century AD

Ceramic oil lamp in the shape of a human foot, only 10cm (4in.) long, wearing an ornate thonged leather shoe with the sole decorated with hobnails in a pattern. The wick for the lamp would have burned in the big toe, where there is a hole and evidence of burning. A hole at the ankle would have been used for filling the lamp with olive oil. From the excavations for the Jubilee Line in Borough High Street, Southwark.

Amphora, AD 70–120

Large ceramic container for fish sauce (an essential ingredient for cooking). Amphorae were used as containers for the long-distance transportation of commodities such as wine, olive oil and fish sauce. This particular amphora bears a faint painted Latin inscription on its neck stating that 'Lucius Tettius Africanus supplies the finest fish sauce from Antibes'. The amphora, when found, contained the remains of the sauce – numerous heads of Spanish mackerel.

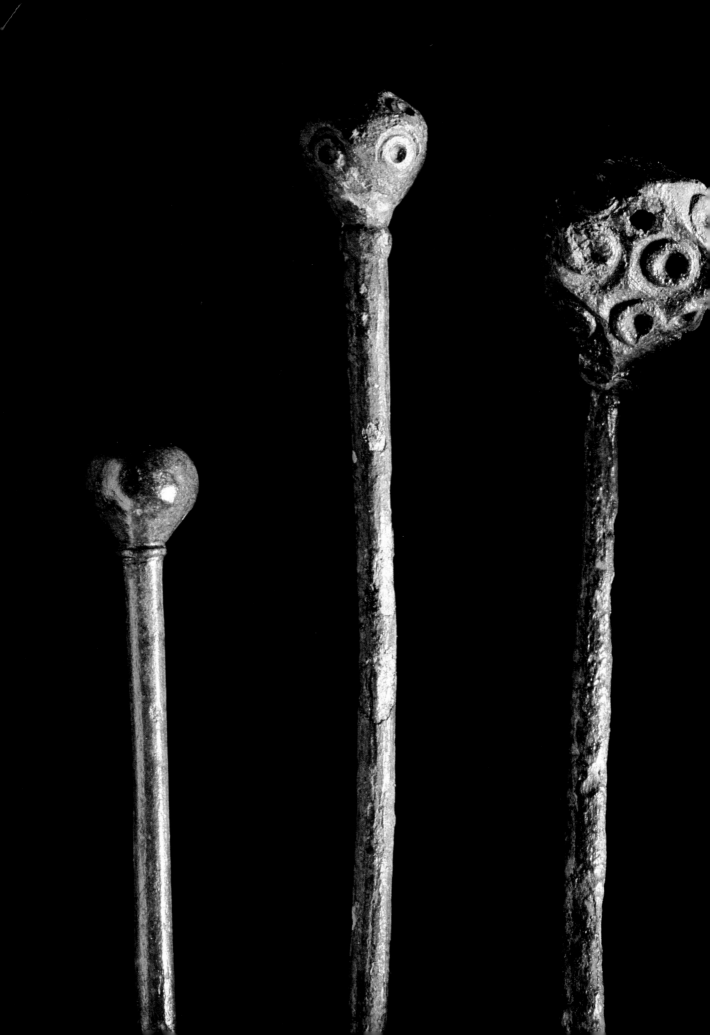

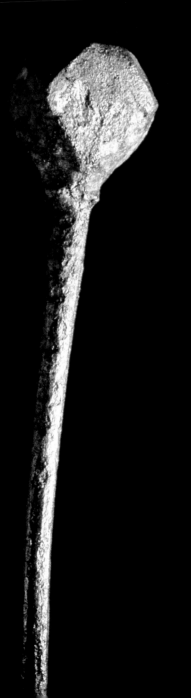

Saxon
London

Dress pins, late 8th to early 9th century
Found during excavations at Shorts
Gardens, near Covent Garden, on the
edge of the site of Lundenwic, these large
pins with decorative heads were used to
fasten the clothes of Saxon Londoners.

Early Saxon jewellery, 6th century
One of the finest objects from the Anglo-Saxon cemetery at Mitcham was this 'square-headed' brooch, cast in silver and then gilded. It was found in the grave of a young woman; lying at her throat, it once fastened the garment in which she was buried. The three 'saucer' brooches are less fine, made of copper alloy (bronze or brass). They were found with Anglo-Saxon burials at Hanwell, west London.

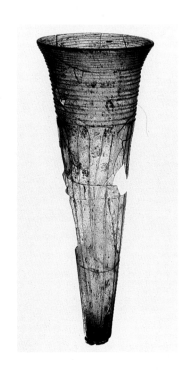

Conical glass beaker, 5th century
Anglo-Saxon settlers in the London area brought with them their own customs, as well as a new culture and new styles of art. Gravegoods were buried with the dead, and reflected the status and wealth their owners had when alive. Glass vessels were rare and highly prized. This glass drinking beaker with trailed decoration was found in an early Saxon burial at Mitcham, south London.

Late Saxon pottery,
10th to early 11th century *(left)*

London in late Saxon times was supplied with ordinary domestic pottery from a number of sources. These vessels, a bowl with a spout and a large spouted jar or pitcher, are made of clay containing tiny fragments of fossil shell characteristic of the upper Thames valley, in Oxfordshire. The pots were probably made somewhere in that area and shipped down the Thames for sale in the markets in London.
in that area and shipped down the Thames for sale in the markets in London.

Cooking pot and loom weights,
8th to 9th century *(above)*

These objects, found during building works in the Strand in 1924–5, were the first finds to be recognised from the district now known to be the site of the Saxon trading town of Lundenwic, which grew up in the 7th and 8th centuries to the west of the ruins of Roman London, along the Strand and around Covent Garden and the Aldwych. Among the most typical finds from this area are ring-shaped weights of baked clay, which were used to tension the warp (vertical) threads on an upright loom. Such looms were to be found in most Anglo-Saxon homes, for weaving woollen cloth – not just for domestic use but for sale, as the good quality of English cloth was already internationally famous.

Group of Viking-age weapons, early 11th century

These elegant iron battle axes and spearheads reflect the troubled period, around AD 1000, when Danish invaders joined forces with the descendants of those Scandinavian vikings who had settled in northern and eastern England, in an attempt to win control of the kingdom. The period culminated in the crowning of the Dane Cnut (Canute) as king of England. London came under direct attack on a number of occasions, and these weapons were found during building works close to the site of the Saxon London Bridge, where the fighting seems to have centred. They may have been lost during a battle, or thrown into the river as a victory offering afterwards.

Penny issued by King Alfred the Great, c. 886

The basic unit of currency throughout most of the Anglo-Saxon and Norman periods was the silver penny. Good-quality coinage was vital to trade and could also carry a political message – like this coin of King Alfred, 18mm (a little less than ¾in.) in diameter. The king's head is modelled on the diademed heads of emperors on Roman coins. On the other side is a monogram made up of the letters LVNDONIA (London). The coin was presumably minted in London after the city came under Alfred's rule, following his battles against the viking invaders, and may have been issued to celebrate his success.

Grave slab, early 11th century

Found in building works near St Paul's Cathedral in 1852, this limestone slab probably once formed part of an impressive tomb monument for a member of the Scandinavian court of King Cnut. It is carved with a stylised beast (a lion) in battle with a serpent, in the so-called 'Ringerike' style of decoration that developed in late Saxon England under the influence of settlers from Scandinavia, and was once richly coloured. Carved on the left-hand end is an inscription in Norse runes – ':KINA:LET:LEKIA:STIN:THENSI:AUK:TUKI:' ('Ginna and Toki had this stone laid').

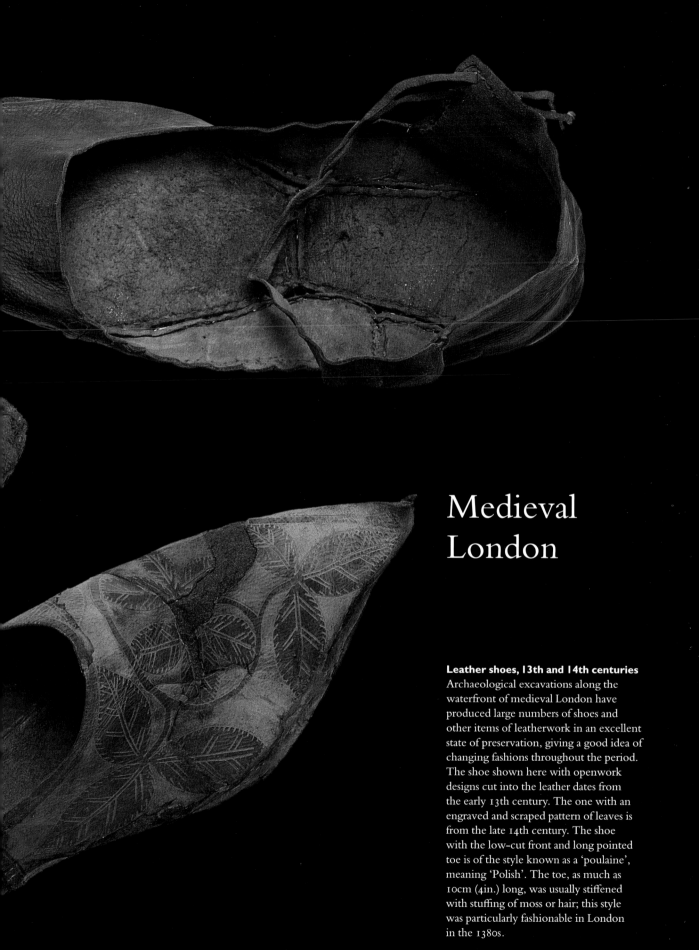

Medieval London

Leather shoes, 13th and 14th centuries
Archaeological excavations along the waterfront of medieval London have produced large numbers of shoes and other items of leatherwork in an excellent state of preservation, giving a good idea of changing fashions throughout the period. The shoe shown here with openwork designs cut into the leather dates from the early 13th century. The one with an engraved and scraped pattern of leaves is from the late 14th century. The shoe with the low-cut front and long pointed toe is of the style known as a 'poulaine', meaning 'Polish'. The toe, as much as 10cm (4in.) long, was usually stiffened with stuffing of moss or hair; this style was particularly fashionable in London in the 1380s.

Heraldic panel, probably from the Great Cross in Cheap, c. 1291–5

In 1290 Eleanor of Castile, the wife of King Edward I, died near Lincoln. Her body was carried in a solemn procession to Westminster Abbey for burial, and the king ordered a monument to be erected at each place where the coffin had rested overnight. Two monuments were set up in London, in Cheapside ('the Great Cross') and at the west end of the Strand ('Charing Cross'). This is one of two slabs of Purbeck marble (a form of limestone) found in 1838 during construction of a sewer in Cheapside. They show the coats of arms of England (*left*) and Castile, and probably came from the Great Cross.

Pottery, late 13th to early 14th century

The Museum of London's collection of medieval pottery is unique. This group of pottery, all found in London, is a small selection of the range of ordinary kitchen and tableware available to Londoners in the late 13th and early 14th centuries. The tall jugs at the back came from kilns close to the medieval city. The small condiment dish and the drinking horn in the foreground and the conical jug with a human face (*left*) were all made at Kingston-upon-Thames, Surrey. The jug with striped decoration (*right*) was made at Mill Green, near Chelmsford, in Essex. The jug in the centre, of fine white clay with painted shields, is from the region of Saintes in western France and probably came to London with the wine trade from Bordeaux.

Pilgrim badges, mid- to late 14th century

The travels of pious Londoners to the shrines of saints and the sites of holy relics are reflected in the vast numbers of badges and mementoes they brought back. Favourite with Londoners was the Canterbury shrine of Thomas Becket, the archbishop murdered in December 1170, who was born and brought up in London. These two badges, mass-produced in a cheap tin-lead alloy, illustrate two aspects of the cult of St Thomas: the commemoration of his return by ship from France shortly before his death, and the jewelled bust that contained a fragment of the saint's skull.

Glass goblet, 14th century

This goblet was found during excavations on the site of Winchester House, Southwark, the London residence of the medieval Bishops of Winchester. Only the wealthy could afford high-quality glass tableware like this. Such good glass was not made in England in the Middle Ages, and this piece was probably imported from Italy or southern France.

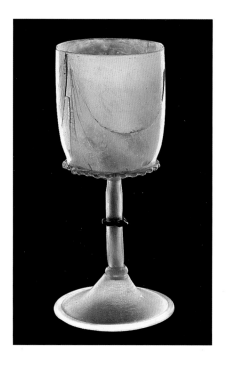

Mayoralty seal, 1381

In 1381 the City commissioned a new seal for the use of the Mayor. The silver matrix was delivered on 17 April 1381 and remained in use for over 500 years until 1913, when – by now very worn – it was replaced by a new seal with a similar design. The seal shows figures of St Paul with a sword and St Thomas Becket in his archbishop's robes. Below is a shield with the City's arms: the cross of St George with the sword of St Paul in one quarter.

Daggers, late 14th to 15th century

The larger of these two civilian daggers is a 'baselard', the type of weapon used in 1381 by the mayor William Walworth to strike down Wat Tyler, leader of the Peasants' Revolt, when King Richard II confronted the rebels in Smithfield.

Spectacle frames, late 14th to early 15th century

Reading glasses were invented in Italy in the 13th century, and were imported into England in large numbers from Flanders and the Netherlands in the late 14th and 15th centuries. Parts of several pairs of frames, made of bone or antler, have been found in recent London excavations. The frames pivot on a metal rivet, so that they could be clipped onto the reader's nose.

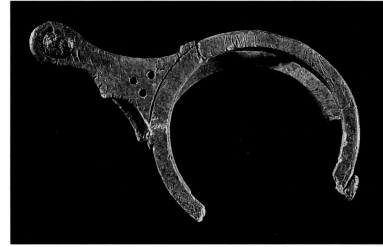

The 'Common Chest', early 15th century

This chest or strongbox, made of iron plates, was kept in the City's Guildhall for many years. It is believed to be the medieval 'Common Chest', made to hold valuables and vital City property. A document dating from 1427 refers to the Chest and its six keys, each of which was held by a member of the City's Corporation. All six men would need to be present to oversee the opening of the chest.

Panel from a wooden chest, c. 1410

This elmwood panel, the right-hand part of the front of a large chest, reflects the work of medieval London's most famous writer, Geoffrey Chaucer. It illustrates a version of a story about the evils of greed that he included in his *Canterbury Tales*. Three youths find a treasure, and two of them stay to guard it while the third goes to buy food and drink to celebrate. Planning to kill his companions for their share of the loot, he poisons the wine (*left*). On his return his similarly minded friends set upon him and murder him (*centre*); they then sit down and drink the poisoned wine (*right*).

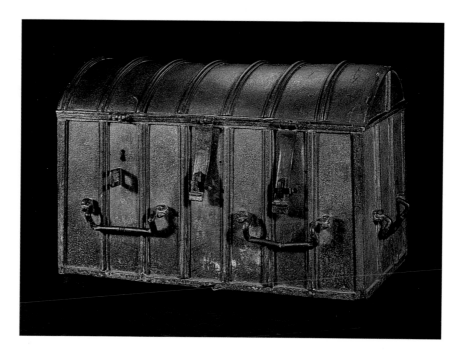

Statues of two 'Virtues', c. 1430

In 1411 work began on the construction of
a new Guildhall as the centre of London's
local government. The building, most of
which still survives in use today, was
largely completed by 1430. The facade of
the main entrance was decorated with
statues in niches. On either side of the
doorway were symbolic figures of four
'Virtues', each trampling a conquered
'Vice'. A later writer identified the figures
as Discipline, Justice, Fortitude and
Temperance – though traditionally the
four cardinal virtues include Prudence, not
Discipline. When the facade was
demolished in 1788, the statues were sold.
After many years in a garden in north
Wales, they returned to London in the
1970s and can be seen in the Museum.
The two figures shown here are thought
to be Discipline and Justice.

Silver collar, c. 1440–50

Collars or necklaces made up of links in
the form of the letter S were bestowed by
the Lancastrian kings Henry IV, Henry V
and Henry VI on their supporters as a
badge of honour. The letter S probably
stood for 'Souverayne' (sovereign), a
motto used by Henry IV. A silver collar
like this would have been worn by a royal
official or ambassador, with a royal or
family badge hanging from the fluted ring
at the bottom.

Reliquary pendant, 15th century

This small gold cross-shaped pendant just 5cm (2in.) high was probably worn on a chain, or possibly hung from a set of rosary beads. On the front is a Crucifixion scene on a background of blue enamel, with garnets set at the end of each arm of the cross; on the back is a picture of the Virgin and Child. The cross hinges at the bottom to reveal a small fragment of wood inside, embedded in wax. This is clearly intended to be a fragment of the True Cross (the actual cross on which Christ was crucified).

Cradle, late 15th century

Made of oak, this was the night cradle of a high-born baby. It swings from posts surmounted by heraldic birds, guarding the sleeping child. Once believed to have been the cradle of the infant Henry V, it is far too late in date ever to have served that purpose. Nevertheless, it is a unique survival of this type of medieval furniture.

Tudor and Stuart London

Watches, 1650–1700
Protestant refugees from the Low
Countries and France, had a huge impact
on London in this period. Many were
skilled craftworkers and set up successful
workshops in their new home.
Left: Watch, *c.* 1700, with verge
escapement with calendar and lunar
indications in a silver case, made by
Thomas Tompion.
Right: Watch, *c.* 1650, with verge
escapement and enamel-and-paste case,
made by Abraham Beckner of Popes
Head Alley.

Reliquary bust of a saint, mid-16th century *(right)*

Reliquaries (receptacles for the relics of saints) were found in most London churches until the Reformation. This bronze reliquary was probably made in Italy. From the Thames at Wapping.

Portable Mass set, hallmarked 1534 *(below)*

The set consists of a silver-gilt chalice which unscrews, a paten (Communion plate) and a glass bottle for wine. It was used by a priest to celebrate Mass with the sick and dying.

Belt chape, c. 1530 *(below right)*

A silver-gilt chape (protective cap for a belt end) with a cast-relief figure of St Barbara and incised motifs of a rose and a pomegranate, the Royal badges of Henry VIII and Katherine of Aragon. The chape has an inverse inscription, RAF+FEL+MIGAM, an abbreviation of the name Ralph Felmingham, who was one of the Sergeant-at-arms of Henry VIII. Felmingham was present at the trial of Lord Dacre in 1534, and that of Anne Boleyn and her brother Lord Rocheford in 1536.

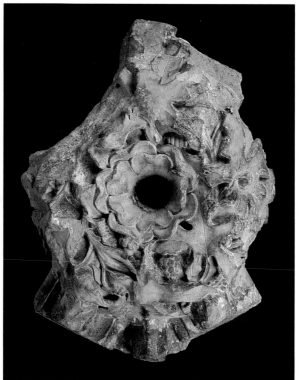

Ceiling boss used as foundation rubble for Nonsuch Palace

This palace was built for Henry VIII between 1538 and 1547. It was constructed on the site of Merton Priory, which was demolished during the Dissolution of the Monasteries earlier in Henry's reign. Some 3600 tons of stone from the medieval priory, including this elaborate ceiling boss, was used as foundation rubble for the palace.

Leather jerkin, c. 1560

A boy's jerkin with pinked (punched) decoration of stars and heart motifs between scored lines. These sleeveless garments were worn over a matching or contrasting doublet to provide extra warmth and protection. Although jerkins were masculine garments, they were practical and occasionally copied in women's fashion; Queen Elizabeth I had two made in 1577, probably for riding.

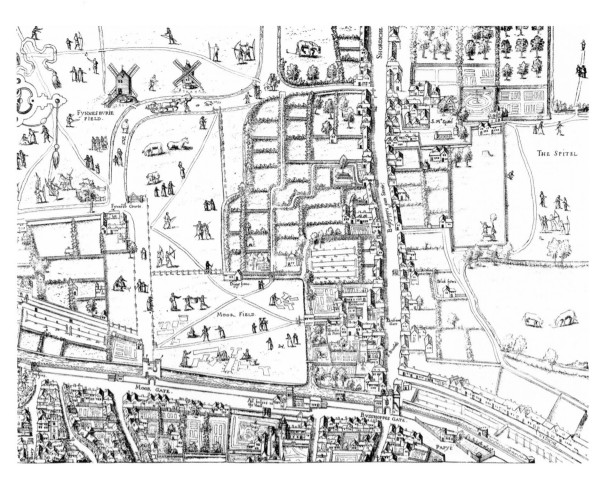

Maps of Moorfields, 1553–9

Two engraved copperplate maps covering a north to south section from Shoreditch to London Bridge. They are the only surviving examples from the original set of fifteen plates which formed the oldest known plan of London. They provide an invaluable insight into the layout and activities of the Tudor city. In the lower map are the densely packed buildings and narrow streets of the central part of the city, together with some of the important riverside sharves. In the upper map, Bishopsgate Street can be seen heading north from the city, and Londoners are pictured in Moorfields drying their washing, practising archery and stretching cloth on 'tenter' frames.

London from Southwark, c. 1630

This anonymous painting is the earliest surviving oil painting with London as its sole subject. It shows the city in one breadth, from Whitehall to the Tower – providing a complete summary of the capital before it was destroyed by the Great Fire.

Pottery vessels, 1580–1620

Excavated from a stone-lined well in the Fleet Valley, the range of vessels includes popular and luxury wares. The pottery was discarded in the mid-17th century.

Trenchers, early 17th century

In affluent households meals sometimes finished with sweetmeats, such as quince cheese, crystallised fruit or marzipan. Trenchers, plain side up, were used as plates. The ones shown here are made of beechwood, painted with floral designs and inscribed with moral maxims.

POST-MEDIEVAL JEWELLERY

During the 16th and early 17th century jewellery was a major component of fashionable attire, and London was the principal centre of luxury trades such as jewellery manufacture. Worn to augment and reflect personal status, jewellery was also regarded as a significant financial asset, and items were frequently pledged as security for loans.

The Cheapside Hoard

A box containing over 230 pieces of jewellery, some of which are shown here, was recovered from the site of Wakefield House, Cheapside in 1912. Thought to be part of a goldsmith's stock-in-trade, the hoard was probably concealed during the Civil War. The jewellery reflects the taste of the prosperous merchant class of the period 1560 to 1640.

Finger-ring, early 17th century

This gold ring is inscribed 'PENCES POUR MOYE DV' ('Think of me, God willing'), with a heart pierced by two arrows. Recovered from excavations (1988–9) of the Rose Theatre, built by Philip Henslowe in 1587.

CIVIL WAR AND COMMONWEALTH COLLECTIONS

A significant and important collection of material relating specifically to Oliver Cromwell and the events of the Commonwealth was acquired by the Museum in 1913 from the family of Sir Richard Tangye. As well as manuscripts and printed books, the Tangye collection includes paintings, portrait miniatures and plaques, medals and other items – among them Cromwell's Bible, funeral escutcheon and death mask.

Cromwell's death mask

A gentleman farmer from Huntingdon, Cromwell became Lieutenant-General of the parliamentary forces during the Civil War and subsequently Lord Protector of England from 1653 until his death. Cromwell gradually assumed all the pomp and style of a king, without the title, taking up residence in Whitehall Palace, where he died on 3 September 1658.

Cavalry flags used as screen panels, mid-17th century (oil on silk)

A set of Civil War royalist cavalry cornets (flags), once fringed and carried by a cavalier attached to a lance. The flags represented a troop of horse. Only two other Civil War cavalry flags are known to survive. On 13 November 1642 the parliamentary troops, including a London contingent, confronted the Royalists at Turnham Green. This was the closest Civil War battle to London. In 1645 some 4000 Royalist prisoners from the Battle of Naseby were housed in the Mews at Charing Cross.

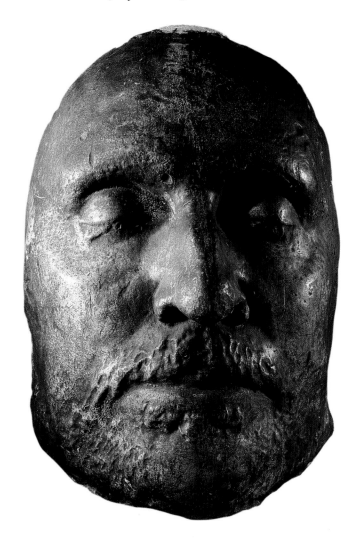

The Great Fire of London, 1666

after Jan Griffer the Elder (c. 1645/52–1718)
The Great Fire of London started in a baker's shop in Pudding Lane in the early hours of Sunday 2 September 1666 and raged for the next four days, destroying four-fifths of the buildings within the city walls. This painting derives from a work by a Dutch artist who came to London soon after the fire. Despite not witnessing the fire at first hand, the artist gives us a strong sense of the cataclysmic scale of the disaster.

The Great Plague, 1665

Group consisting of mortality bill, iron bell, and a spoon and plate commemorating the last major epidemic of plague in London. At its peak in 1665, the number of recorded deaths in London and the suburbs exceeded 7000 per week, as reported in the weekly mortality bills. The scale of suffering is revealed by the inscription on the silver-gilt spoon, which reads 'when died at London of the plague 68,596 of all diseases 97, 306'. The iron bell was rung to announce the collection of the dead, and by the end of the year, some twenty-five per cent of London's population had died.

The Frozen Thames Looking Eastwards towards Old London Bridge, 1677

Abraham Hondius (c. 1625/30–91)

This is one of the earliest paintings of the Thames frozen from bank to bank, an event that occurred regularly until the demolition of the old London Bridge in 1828 increased the speed of the current. This painting shows the frost around New Year 1677, when the ice was not sufficiently thick to allow fairs or events to be held, but people were able to cross the frozen river on foot.

Coronation mug, 1660–1

Commemorative tin-glazed earthenware with a portrait of Charles II, probably made in London. This is possibly the earliest example of commemorative pottery, and celebrates the Restoration of Charles II in 1660. The turbulent events of the mid-17th century inspired potters to produce commemorative wares.

Gerard the Giant, 17th century

A house sign of painted wood from Gerard's Hall in Basing Lane, in the City. The house was destroyed in the Great Fire of London. It was rebuilt as a tavern and demolished in 1852 for the development of Cannon Street.

Virginals, 1656

Inscribed 'JACOBUS WHITE FECIT 1656', this instrument was made by one of the most important virginal-making workshops in 17th century England. James White worked in Old Jewry and became a Freeman of the Joiners' Company in 1656.

Arms of the Hanseatic League, 1670

The Steelyard in Thames Street was the London headquarters of the Hanseatic League, a powerful network of German merchants. These arms were carved by Caius Cibber (1630–1700) for the new Steelyard, which was rebuilt after the Great Fire of London. A sculptor of some renown, Cibber received the sum of £5 from the City of London for this work.

The *London* Cup, 1670

Silver-gilt cup and cover commemorating the launch of HMS *London*, given by the City to replace a ship blown up in 1664. The arms are those of James, Duke of York as Lord High Admiral. The *London* weighed 1338 tons, and had 94 guns and a crew of 750.

Bodice, 1645–55

An elegant tailored garment of pale blue moiré (watered) silk, originally lined with a thick linen twill and whalebone (baleen) stays. The bodice is enhanced by jewellery from the late 17th or early 18th century. The necklace and earrings are of *coque de perles* (pieces of nautilus shell), backed with mother-of-pearl, in gilt metal collets with green pastes and a seed-pearl bow.

Tin-glazed plate, late 17th century

Tin-glazed earthenware, decorated with half-length portraits of King William and Queen Mary and inscribed 'WMR'. The events of the so-called 'Glorious Revolution' forced James II to abdicate in 1689. William III was offered the English throne by a convocation of parliament, but only in conjunction with his wife Mary, the eldest daughter of James II and nearest Protestant claimant to the English throne.

Crown frame, 1685

Worn by Mary of Modena (1658–1718), second wife of James II, at her coronation in 1685. The crown frame, of gilt copper alloy, was designed and made by Richard de Beauvoir. The original setting has been replaced by paste diamonds and imitation pearls.

18th-century London

Anne Fanshawe's dress, c. 1751

This spectacular dress is made from
brocaded silk, woven in Spitalfields.
The dress was made for Anne Fanshawe,
the daughter of Crisp Gascoyne, a
merchant who became Lord Mayor of
London in 1752. Family tradition has it
that Anne acted as her father's hostess and
this dress was made for her to wear on
ceremonial occasions.

Figures of charity-school children, early 18th century

These two statues were erected on Baynard Castle Ward School, near Blackfriars, in the City. Like many charity-school children, the pupils wore uniforms of blue coats and yellow stockings, which were said to frighten away rats.

Two dresses c. 1770–8, doll c. 1750

The two figures and the doll are dressed in printed linen, an alternative to woven silk. The fabrics may have been printed by London firms.

The Blackett Baby House', c. 1760

This large doll's house was given to the London Museum in 1912 by a Miss Blackett. Much of the detail mirrors what would have been found in a real London house of the period. The one exception is the location of the kitchen.

John Middleton with his family in his drawing room, c. 1796–7

John Middleton was one of London's leading 'colourmen', a supplier of paints and pigments to artists and house painters. He had a shop in St Martin's Lane and is shown here holding an emblem of his trade – a book of pigments. The artist of this portrait is not known: Middleton family tradition has it that the work was painted in order to discharge a debt for artist's materials.

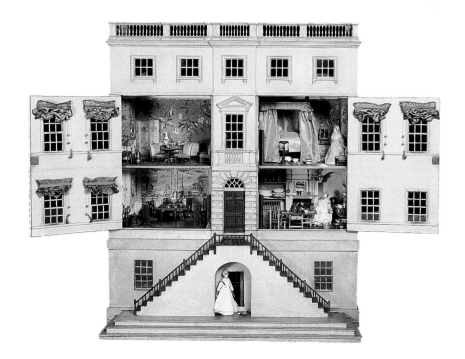

Panelling from Wellclose Square prison
This panelling from an 18th-century prison cell bears names and inscriptions carved by some of the inmates. Wellclose Square, near the Tower of London, was a small prison converted from an ordinary house.

Jack Sheppard, 1724
Sir James Thornhill (1675–1734)
The robber Jack Sheppard was one of London's most celebrated 18th-century criminals, famous for his escapes from Newgate Gaol. Following his fourth recapture he was restrained in his cell with 300 pounds (nearly 150 kilos) of chains, before being hung for his crimes in November 1724.

'Curds and Whey', c. 1730

British School

In this striking and sinister picture three young chimney sweeps are buying a dish of curds from a country dairy maid, who may be blind. The scene is set at the end of Milk Street, off Cheapside, a place where chimney sweeps congregated.

Nightman's brass plaque

This small plaque is a reminder that 18th-century London lacked mains drainage. Nightmen, or night-soil men, provided an essential service by emptying cesspits and disposing of unpleasant household waste, usually by night. The waste was collected in special carts and taken to 'lay-stalls', huge refuse heaps, to compost down into manure for market gardeners.

Cutlery

Examples of cutlery in common use in 18th-century London. The pewter spoon shows the heads of King George III and Queen Charlotte. The fork was found on the Thames foreshore in the 1980s.

Stomacher brooch, 1760s

Bow-shaped brooches, worn on the dress front, were popular in the second half of the 18th century. This example is made from high-quality pastes set in silver alloy. The case is original and is made of paper treated to resemble sharkskin.

May Morning, c. 1760

John Collet (1725–80)

John Collet, a follower of Hogarth, recorded scenes of London life. The event shown here is an old folk custom whereby on the first day of May servants dressed in outlandish clothes, and milkmaids wore headdresses made from pieces of silver and household goods. The revellers in Collet's portrait include a hurdy-gurdy player and a Black servant – a rare confirmation of the presence of Black people in London during the 18th century.

Watts' 'Improved Pocket Lantern', 1790s

Patented by Watts, chemists and druggists of 478 Strand, this neat apparatus is a reminder that candles and oil lamps were the only sources of light during the hours of darkness. It is designed to fit in a pocket when collapsed and includes a small drawer for spare candles.

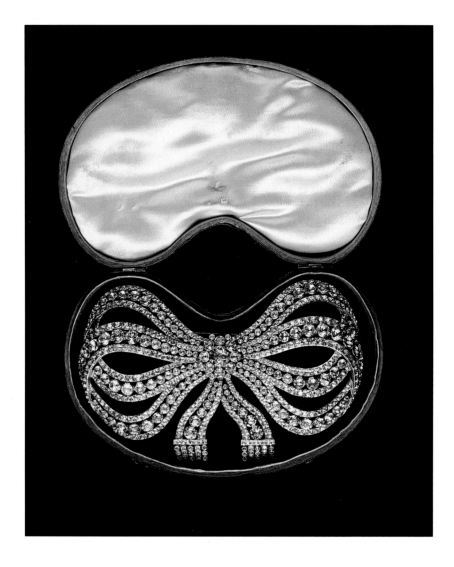

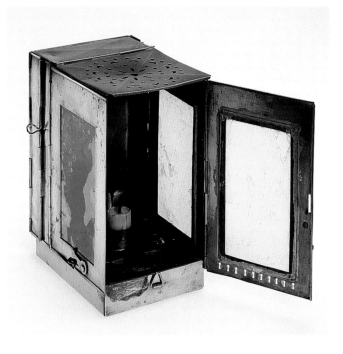

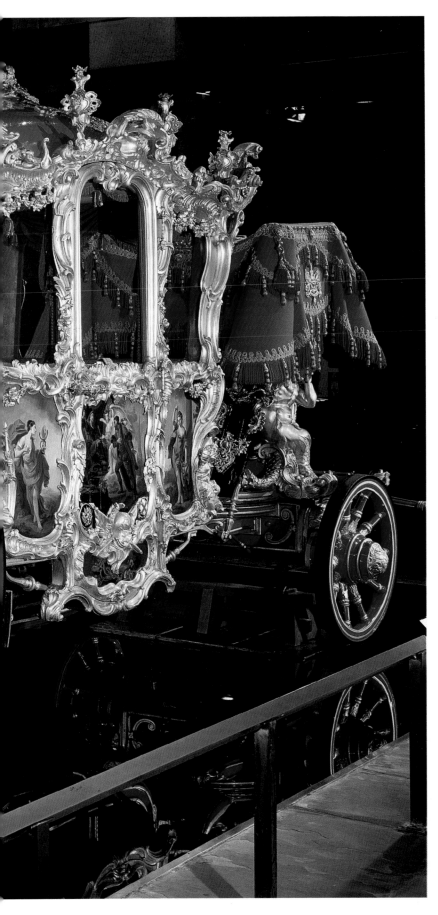

The Lord Mayor's Coach, c. 1757

The Lord Mayor of London's Coach is one of the Museum's most memorable exhibits. It remains the property of the Corporation of London and is taken out of the Museum once a year for the Lord Mayor's Show. The coach is a masterpiece of virtuoso craftsmanship. Formally commissioned in 1757, it was first used in the Lord Mayor's Parade of that year. The design is by Sir Robert Taylor, and the construction would have involved a number of different craftsmen – notably carvers, gilders and painters. The paintings, which are elaborate allegories associating London's commercial might with virtuousness, are attributed to an Italian painter, Battista Cipriani, who arrived in London from Rome in 1755.

18TH-CENTURY MANUFACTURES

London in the 18th century contained thousands of workshops and manufacturing concerns. Trades tended to congregate in certain districts: clockmaking and watchmaking were carried on in Clerkenwell, silk-weaving took place in Spitalfields. Industrial processes that needed water, such as textile printing, were located on the banks of the Thames or its tributaries.

The Museum has many examples of items made in London during the 18th century. It has good holdings of luxury goods: porcelain, fine table glass, jewellery, enamels, watchmaking. Decorative items of this sort were given in quantity to the London Museum by its early benefactors, notably J.G. Joicey. More recently the Museum has tried to balance its collections with examples of London manufactures intended for more everyday use.

Panel of printed linen and cotton, 1769
(above left)
Robert Jones & Co.
Robert Jones owned a textile-printing works at Old Ford, near Bow. This fabric was intended for household furnishings. Unusually, the manufacturer has incorporated his own name in the design.

Dress panel of woven silk, 1707–8
(above right)
A wide range of silk fabrics was woven in the Spitalfields area, to the east of the City. Some of the weavers were Protestant refugees from northern Europe, others were from England and Ireland, attracted to London by the promise of work. Spitalfields silk is recognisable by its designs.

Pocket telescope, mid 18th century
John Cuff
Cuff was a leading optical-instrument maker with premises in Fleet Street, 'At the Sign of the Reflecting Microscope & Spectacles'. Making optical and mathematical instruments was a highly skilled trade, located almost entirely in central London.

Pair of shoes

These silk shoes are rare examples of 18th-century shoes known to have been made in London. According to the printed label inside the shoe they were made by 'Francis Poole, Women's Shoemaker, in the old Change near Cheapside'. They date from the 1760s and were made for a 'Miss Ellis', whose name is written inside.

Enamel souvenir boxes, mid-18th century

An enamelling workshop operated at Battersea between 1753 and 1756. Enamelling was a speciality of the West Midlands, and it is possible that these boxes, despite their obvious connection with London, were made there and shipped to London for sale.

THE PRINTED EPHEMERA COLLECTION

The 18th century saw a vast increase in the amount of printed material circulating in London. In 1725 there were 75 printing offices in the city. Sixty years later this had increased to 124. Printing transformed the speed with which information travelled, and the type of information produced.

The London Museum collected printed ephemera from its early days. The Guildhall Museum's interest was less strong, since it was collecting in partnership with the Guildhall Library, to which it referred all printed material. Today the Museum of London's collection of printed ephemera contains 250,000 items, covering similar ground to the larger London ephemera collection held at the Guildhall Library. The Museum has particularly strong collections of trade cards, early almanacs, playbills and playscripts.

Trade card for Richard Harper, nightman, 18th century

Trade cards served as bills, receipts and advertisements for the wares or services provided by specialist tradesmen and tradeswomen.

Cloe, as sung at the publick Gardens

A souvenir of a popular song of the day, intended for use at home or at one of London's pleasure gardens, such as Vauxhall or Ranelagh.

A hint to the Ladies to take care of their Heads, 1776

This is a satire on the outrageously tall wigs worn by ladies of fashion in the 1770s. The background shows a view of the Pantheon, a glamorous rendezvous which is also the subject of an oil painting in the Museum's collection. The site, to the east of Oxford Circus, is now occupied by Marks & Spencer.

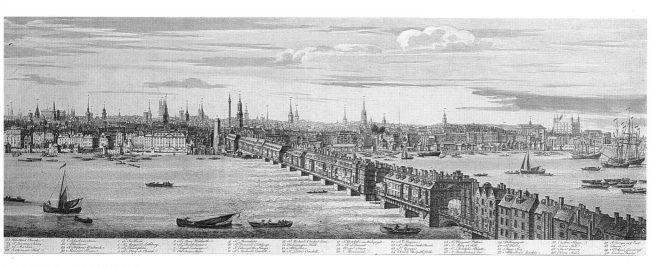

TOPOGRAPHICAL VIEWS

Views of London's changing cityscape form the backbone of the paintings, prints and drawings collection. The production of such views multiplied in the 18th century, reflecting both the scale of building activity and the growing market for pictures as souvenirs.

The subject matter of the city scenes recorded by 18th-century artists and printmakers tended to be the new developments, the new residential squares, churches, bridges, markets and streets. Besides recording the appearance of streets and buildings, artists often tried to convey the extraordinary 'busy-ness' of London. London was bigger and more complex than any other British city. To contemporary eyes, its vast expanse of buildings and variety of human activity would have seemed remarkable.

Panorama of the City of London, 1749

engraved by Samuel Buck (1696–1779)
This is one section of a panorama recording the extent of the cities of London and Westminster. This half shows the eastern side of the City and the old London Bridge, just before the removal of its houses.

Blackfriars Bridge, 1798

Nathaniel Black (active 1790s) and Thomas Rowlandson for the figures
This large watercolour was exhibited at the Royal Academy in 1801. It shows the bridge, opened in 1769, carrying a variety of human and animal traffic. Note the Lord Mayor's barge in the distance.

The Adelphi, 1771–2 *(above left)*
William Marlow (1740–1813)
The Adelphi was an ambitious riverside development of twenty-four grand town houses conceived by the Adam brothers and requiring an enabling Act of Parliament to permit the enclosure of the river bank. This painting, showing the half-completed development, was presented to the London Museum by the American financier J. Pierpoint Morgan in 1923.

Covent Garden Market, 1770–80 *(below left)*
John Collet (1725–80)
Covent Garden was originally laid out as a residential square, but this painting shows the activity for which it became famous from the late 17th century onwards – selling fruit and vegetables. Here, the south side of the square has been taken over permanently by stalls and greenhouses.

St George's Church, Hanover Square, 1785–95 *(above right)*
Thomas Malton, Jr (1748–1817)
This church was one of sixty new London churches erected after 1711 with financial encouragement from the government. St George's, designed by John James and built in 1721–4, was the first London church to have an entrance with a full-size classical portico. It became one of London's most fashionable places of worship.

Bird's-eye View of the West India Docks, 1802 *(below right)*
aquatint by William Daniel (1769–1837)
The West India Docks were opened in 1802 as London's first purpose-built trading docks. They were constructed on a vast scale to cater for a trading operation of unprecedented ambition as goods from the West Indies arrived in quantity in London, often to be shipped on to other European ports.

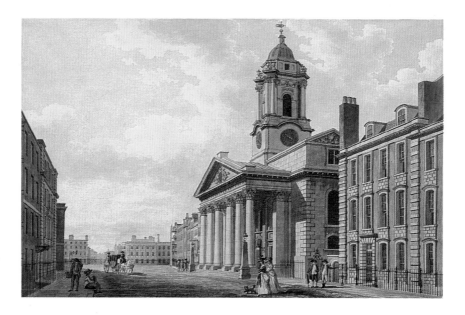

19th-century London

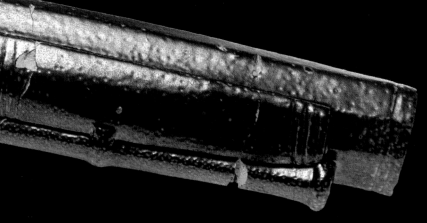

Two stoneware jugs and a pistol flask, early 19th century

The two jugs commemorate popular heroes of the early 19th century: Lord Nelson (left) and the Duke of Wellington (right). All three pieces were made at Lambeth. The Nelson jug was made by the firm Doulton & Watts, the Wellington jug and flask by Stephen Green.

Model of the Lord Mayor's Barge, 1807

This large scale model of the City barge was supplied by its builders, Searle & Godfrey of Stangate, Lambeth. Lovingly finished and decorated, this 80-foot-long vessel – whose fine lines show its origins in the Thames wherries – was rowed by eighteen watermen. The barge was last used for the Lord Mayor's procession in 1856, ending a 400 year-old tradition.

Waterman's coat, c. 1840

This coat was part of the sumptuous ceremonials that took place on the Thames until the middle of the last century. Many of the City livery companies kept ceremonial barges for festive occasions, such as Lord Mayor's Day. The buttons on the coat shown here carry the coat of arms of the Goldsmiths' Company.

The Falcon Glasshouse at Southwark c.1840

This painting shows the interior of London's largest glasshouse and its teams of skilled craftsmen at work. The Falcon Glasshouse, which was owned by Apsley Pellatt, produced high-quality table glass.

Porcelain plate, early 19th century

The *trompe l'œil* decoration on this plate shows several bills from Pellatt & Green, a firm of china and glass retailers linked to Pellatt's glasshouse at Southwark. It was probably painted as an advertising novelty or as a sample of the work of a china-decorating workshop.

The City from Bankside, 1820s

Thomas Miles Richardson (1784–1848)
St Paul's Cathedral appears in many paintings of this period, but this view of the cathedral is unusual for its emphasis on London's riverside and commercial activity. The working equipment in the foreground and the newly built warehouses on the opposite bank are painted with careful attention to detail.

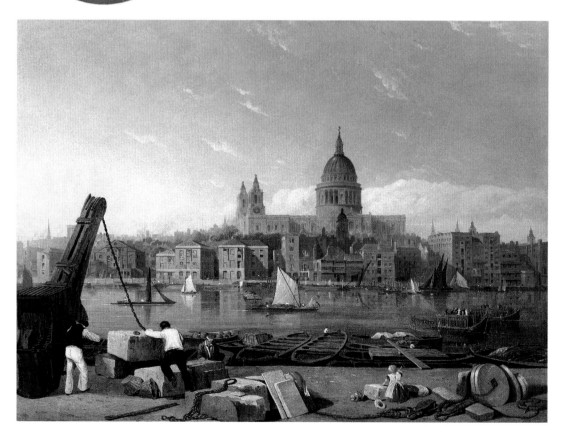

A Funeral Bearer

Robert William Buss (1804–74)
Funeral bearers, or 'mutes', were
employed by undertakers to lead funeral
processions. The white sash worn by the
mute in this portrait indicates that he was
dressed for a child's funeral. The figure in
its companion portrait wears a black sash.

Tiny the Wonder

This printed handkerchief (*c.* 1850) is a
reminder that cruel sports were once a part
of London culture. Tiny the Wonder was
the champion rat-catching terrier at the
Blue Anchor Tavern in Finsbury. Despite
weighing only 5½ pounds (2.5 kilos), he
had a ferocious temperament and on two
occasions killed two hundred barn rats
within an hour. The Museum also has an
oil painting of Tiny the Wonder in action.

Charles Dickens's chair

Several portrait photographs of Charles Dickens taken around 1859, while he was writing *A Tale of Two Cities*, show him sitting in this chair. The chair carries a silver plate engraved with its history. Dickens gave it to a friend, after which it passed through the hands of several collectors and was eventually presented to the London Museum.

The General Post Office, One Minute to Six, 1860

George Elgar Hicks (1824–1914)

The scene is set in the General Post Office in St Martin's le Grand just before closing time on a Friday evening, when the newspapers arrived. It captures the rush of last-minute customers, and the crowd of spectators who came to watch: the 'penny post' had been introduced in 1840 and was still a novelty.

Westminster Abbey and the Palace of Westminster under construction, c. 1857
Roger Fenton (1819–69)
This print is one of the Museum's earliest photographic views of London. Fenton, a founder member of the Photographic Society of London (later the Royal Photographic Society), helped establish photography as a documentary medium through his poignant photographs of the aftermath of the Crimean War. Here he records a city view being transformed by the building of the new Palace of Westminster. The clock tower of the new palace, 'Big Ben', is clearly visible behind the abbey.

Souvenir box and season ticket to The Great Exhibition, 1851
The most spectacular exhibition staged in London during the 19th century was 'The Great Exhibition of the Industry of All Nations', held in 1851. Many of the souvenirs sold to the six million visitors carry pictures of the temporary glass building in which the exhibition was housed, popularly known as the 'Crystal Palace'.

Exhibition clock, 1862
William Davis & Sons
This clock was one of the exhibits shown at the International Exhibition held in London in 1862. It was displayed by a firm of London clockmakers, and shows the time and date in London and eight other world cities. It was presented to the London Museum by J.G. Joicey.

From Pentonville Road Looking West: Evening, 1884

John O'Connor (1830–89)

The main focus of this painting is St Pancras station and the Midland Railway hotel. The hotel, designed by George Gilbert Scott, was opened in 1873, and its picturesque Gothic bulk has dominated this part of London ever since. O'Connor's atmospheric view includes the horse-drawn trams travelling between the Angel and King's Cross, a route introduced in 1884.

Bloomsbury Central Baptist Church, 1885

Herbert Marshall (1841–1913)

The church was built in 1845–8 as the principal church of the English Baptist movement. This watercolour gives a good impression of the more relaxed state of London streets before the arrival of the motor car. The spires were removed in 1951.

THE ROYAL COLLECTIONS

The London Museum of 1911 was devised partly as a memorial to Edward VII, and its early collecting was influenced by the patronage of the Royal Family. Many loans and gifts came from the royal household, particularly from Queen Mary, the wife of King George V. During the 1920s and 1930s much of this material was displayed in special 'Royal Rooms' at Lancaster House, the Museum's home from 1914 to 1943.

The royal collections included pottery and porcelain, royal memorabilia, official gifts and personal items, but the most popular exhibits were the coronation robes and court dresses. In recent years the ceremonial costume has been transferred to the Historic Royal Palaces Agency, to join the court dress collection at Kensington Palace. The Museum of London retains items that illustrate the influence of royalty on the development of London.

Dress worn by Princess Charlotte, 1816–17

This dress belonged to Princess Charlotte (1796–1817) – the daughter and heir of George IV – who died young, in childbirth. The dress is made from olive silk trimmed with artificial pearls, and the style is highly fashionable. A number of Princess Charlotte's dresses survive.

Queen Victoria's dolls, 1831–3

These dolls are part of the large collection of wooden dolls that belonged to the young Princess Victoria, who made some of their dresses with her governess, Baroness Lehzen. Most of the dolls represent ladies from the nobility – but some were dressed as famous ballet dancers and opera singers, whom the Princess much admired.

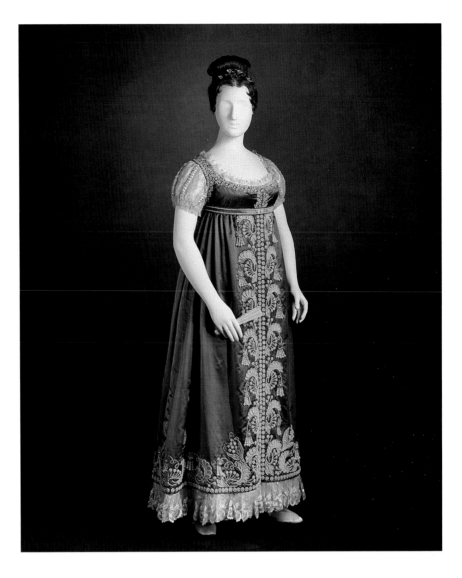

19TH-CENTURY SOCIAL CONCERN

The 19th century saw growing concern about the dark side of London. Poverty, misery and disease were nothing new, but 19th-century opinion found these facts of metropolitan life increasingly intolerable. Details of the squalor found in some areas of the city were made public by writers such as Henry Mayhew and Charles Dickens, whose stories reflected real lives and conditions.

The Museum has little in its collection that directly illustrates the experience of being poor in 19th-century London. What does survive tends to be from the institutions that were formed as a response to poverty. However, paintings and photographs reflect something of the social concern of the period.

Shaftesbury, or Lost and Found, 1862
(left)
William MacDuff (active 1844–76)
A young shoeblack and a street urchin are gazing into the window of a print shop and pointing to an engraving of Lord Shaftesbury (1801–85). Shaftesbury was responsible for many initiatives to improve the lot of London's street children, including the establishment of the Shoe Black Brigade and the Ragged School Union.

A Poor House, c. 1869 *(below left)*
Gustave Doré (1832–83)
Gustave Doré's illustrations to the book
London A Pilgrimage, issued in parts from
1872, showed readers dramatic scenes
of the conditions found in overcrowded
areas of London, notoriously Whitechapel
in the East End. This is one of the few oil
paintings Doré executed on the subject.

Behind the Bar, 1882 *(above right)*
John Henry Henshall (1856–1928)
In this watercolour the artist has included
several details that reflect Victorian
concern about alcohol: a woman feeding
a baby with gin, a child peeping over
the bar, a pawnbroker's sign in the
background. Although carrying
a moral message, the unsentimental
detail of the pub interior gives this
strong work a realistic feel.

Hookey Alf *(below right)*
John Thomson (1837–1921)
In the late 1870s the photographer John
Thomson and the writer Adolphe Smith
issued a publication in parts entitled *Street
Life in London*. This combined striking
photographs of the poor with polemical
essays by Smith. By using photographs
and basing the essays on interviews with
real people, Smith and Thomson insisted
that their reports were not exaggerated.
The scene shown here was photographed
in Whitechapel. In Smith's words:
'There is no sight to be seen in the
streets of London more pathetic than
this oft repeated story – the little child
leading home a drunken parent.'

Hansom cab, late 19th century

The London Museum acquired its first hansom in 1912, at a time when these horse-drawn cabs were still operating on London streets. Hansoms first appeared as vehicles for public hire in the 1830s. They became a familiar sight around the city, with drivers notorious for their rudeness. By 1912 they were rapidly being replaced by motorised taxi cabs.

Model butcher's shop, 1880s

Miniature butcher's shops were popular toys for well-to-do Victorian children. This example includes a Christmas and New Year message.

Colour box, c. 1880

James Reeves & Co.
Reeves is a good example of a London firm whose success was based on one specialist product: in Reeves's case, watercolour pigments pressed into solid cakes. Reeves was established in 1766. This box dates from around 1880, by which time the firm had a large factory at Dalston. It is part of a collection of watercolour boxes given by Reeves to the Museum in 1974.

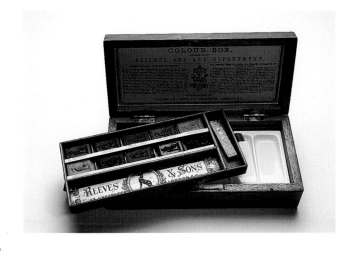

Martinware pottery, 1877–1907

The three Martin Brothers were craft potters, working from a small pottery in Southall. Their grotesque pots appealed to connoisseurs of the day, including Mr Ball Green of Kensington, who gave these pieces to the London Museum in 1922.

Whitefriars glass, 1870–1900

These are typical of the delicate handblown glasses made by the firm of James Powell & Sons at their Whitefriars glasshouse in the City. The firm began making glass in 1834, and by this period enjoyed a reputation for high-quality workmanship and artistic design.

Day dress, c. 1875
Bearing the label of a court dressmaker, Madame Elise of Regent Street, this is an example of a good-quality made-to-measure dress of the period. The seams are machine-stitched, but the dress is finished by hand with 11 metres (12 yards) of trimming. Madame Elise came to public notice in 1863 when one of her seamstresses died, the death being directly attributable to long working hours and poor working conditions.

Women's stockings, 1870–90
All these stockings were given to the museum by members of the public.

Cape, 1893–4
This cape was made for Liberty & Co., the Regent Street shop known for its promotion of progressive and aesthetic fashions. The sinuous patterns and muted colours on this cape are typical of this taste.

The Bayswater Omnibus, 1895
George William Joy (1844–1925)
This painting shows a variety of Londoners sitting together on an omnibus. In the artist's words: 'In the farthest corner sits a poor anxious mother of children, her foot propped on an untidy bundle; beside her, full of kindly thoughts about her, sits a fashionable young woman; next to her the City man, absorbed in his paper; whilst a little milliner, band-box in hand, pressed past the blue-eyed, wholesome-looking nurse in the door way.' Horse-drawn omnibuses first appeared in London in the 1830s.

THE THEATRE COLLECTIONS

The Museum has strong collections of material related to theatre and entertainment in London. The foundations of the theatre collections were laid in 1912 when a band of theatre enthusiasts attempted to turn the new London Museum into a national home for theatrical material. Several distinguished actors lent their support, and the museum was given large quantities of playbills, playscripts, costumes and memorabilia from famous actors. Later curators developed the Museum's interest in entertainment to include music hall, comedy, popular spectacles and cinema. Sport is less well represented in the collections.

Popularity: The Stars of the Edwardian Music Hall, 1901–3

Walter H. Lambert (1870–1950)

This vast group portrait includes 231 of the leading stars of the Edwardian music hall, including Dan Leno, Harry Lauder, Marie Lloyd, the male impersonator Vesta Tilley, and Little Tich. The painter Walter Lambert was also a music-hall performer and included himself in his stage role as a female impersonator called Lydia Dreams. For many years this painting hung in the Castle Hotel in Tooting High Street; it was then bought by Bernard Coleman, who presented it to the London Museum in 1957.

Typical programmes from the Alhambra Palace of Varieties, c. 1900

'The Handsomest Music Hall in Europe' was housed in a building that opened in 1854. It subsequently underwent many transformations under different owners in order to cater for different types of popular entertainment. The building was demolished in 1936, and the Odeon, Leicester Square built on the site.

Clown's suit, 19th century

This costume was thought to have been
worn by Joseph Grimaldi, the famous
London clown, but some of the materials
from which it is made post-date his death
in 1837. It is, however, typical of the
outfits worn by clowns until the early
20th century.

20th-century London

'Arkitex' toy, 1960s
A toy designed to appeal to young would-be architects – who, according to the package, would 'find these construction kits a perfect outlet for their own ideas'.

Sweated Industries Exhibition, 1906
This poster advertises an exhibition organised by the *Daily News* which aimed to draw public attention to the exploitation of low-paid women workers, particularly those in the clothing industry.

Lewis & Allenby design, c. 1900
This design illustrates the fashionable but painful ideal of a tiny wasp waist. Lewis & Allenby specialised in high-quality silks. They were taken over by Dickins & Jones in the early 20th century.

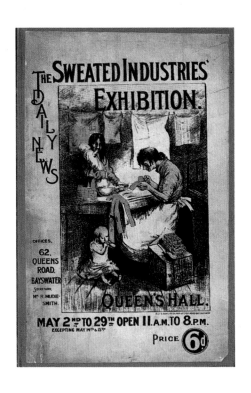

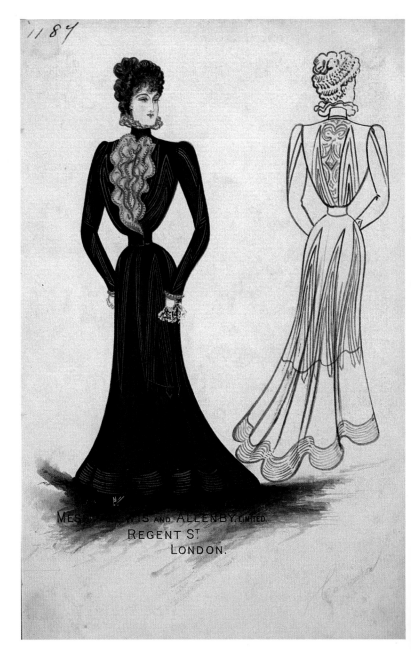

Recruiting poster, First World War

This poster was acquired by the Museum during the First World War as part of a deliberate effort to collect contemporary material illustrating London's experience of wartime: much of this material was later passed to the Imperial War Museum. The image of St Paul's with searchlights was to reappear many times during the Second World War.

Glass-lens workshop, c. 1910

Campbell Gray (active 1900–10)
The gold spectacle frame and eyeglass shop at Theodore Hamblin's premises, 31 New Cavendish Street, W1. Much of London's traditional industrial activity was concerned with the small-scale manufacture of specialised products in workshops like this, and particular areas of London often became closely associated with specific trades and industries.

IT IS FAR BETTER TO FACE THE BULLETS THAN TO BE KILLED AT HOME BY A BOMB

JOIN THE ARMY AT ONCE & HELP TO STOP AN AIR RAID

GOD SAVE THE KING

THE SUFFRAGETTE COLLECTION

In 1948 the Museum was offered a large collection of material belonging to the Suffragette Fellowship. Much of the material consisted of printed or archive material relating to the votes-for-women campaign mounted before the First World War. In addition to posters, newspapers and photographs, the collection contained costume, banners, personal memorabilia, and evocative relics from prison hunger strikes. The presence of the Suffragette Fellowship archive at the Museum attracted donations of further material relating to women's suffrage, and the collection is now widely used by researchers.

Suffragette banner, c. 1910

From the Hammersmith branch of the Women's Social and Political Union, which campaigned for women's suffrage with the motto 'Deeds not Words'. The colours purple, white and green were suffragette colours – signifying integrity, purity and hope.

Suffragette commemorative plaque

Ernestine Mills (1879–1959)

This plaque was enamelled by Ernestine Mills, an artist and metalworker. It commemorates the activities of Georgina, Marie and Hilda Brackenbury, who offered their house as a nursing home for suffragettes released from prison on health grounds after hunger strikes.

Mrs Pankhurst being arrested, 21 May 1914

This famous photograph shows Mrs Pankhurst, one of the leaders of the Women's Social and Political Union, being arrested outside Buckingham Palace after attempting to present a petition to King George V.

May. 21. 1914

Carabosse, the Evil Fairy, 1921
This eye-catching costume was designed
by Leon Bakst for Diaghilev's production
of *The Sleeping Princess* in 1921. The
production was said to be the most exotic
ballet production ever seen in London.

Wembley poster, 1925 *(right)*
designed by C. R. W. Nevinson (1889–1946)
This poster advertises the 1924–5 British
Empire Exhibition at Wembley, and
shows the Amusement Park.

Memory studies, 1923–4 *(below left)*
Vera Wheeler (active 1920s)
Vera Wheeler was a student at the Design
School of the Royal College of Art during
the 1920s. These sketches picture some of
the characters she encountered while out
and about in London.

Woolworth's counter, mid 20th century
(below right)
Woolworth's opened their first London
shop in 1910 and expanded to most
London high streets during the interwar
years. The company slogan was 'Nothing
in this store over 6d'.

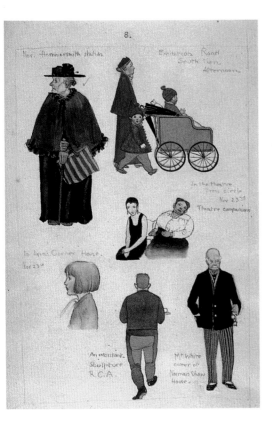

Objects from the Blitz, 1940–4 *(right)*
The Blitz had a profound effect on people who lived through it, and many preserved souvenirs of the event. Some of these objects came to the Museum with vivid personal stories attached to them.

Women in a Tube Shelter, 1944 *(below)*
Henry Moore (1898–1986)
The inspiration for this watercolour was the sight of long-suffering Londoners sleeping in improvised shelters in tube stations during the Blitz.

Moorgate Underground Station
(opposite, above)
Arthur Cross and Fred Tibbs
Cross and Tibbs were City of London police constables who undertook photographic work as part of their official duties. Between 1940 and 1945 they were given the task of recording the devastation caused to the City by air raids. It was thought that photographs might help the task of post-war reconstruction.

Evening in the City of London, 1944
(opposite, below)
David Bomberg (1890–1957)
This painting records a scene of devastation, yet its warm tones give an optimistic feel to the bomb-damaged City. Bomberg took his view from the tower of St Mary-Le-Bow in Cheapside.

Model of the South Bank Exhibition site, 1951

The South Bank Exhibition was part of the 1951 Festival of Britain, which celebrated the nation's recovery after the Second World War. More than eight million festival-goers visited the exhibition and marvelled at futuristic structures and buildings, including the Royal Festival Hall, the Dome of Discovery and the Skylon. This model was made for the exhibition and was given to the Museum after travelling the country as part of the festival celebrations.

The Lansbury Estate, 1951

This poster advertises the showpiece Lansbury Estate at Poplar, erected by the London County Council as the 'Architecture Exhibition' of the Festival of Britain. The estate was named after the East End Labour politician George Lansbury and embodied all the latest thinking about town planning and social housing.

Youths looking in a clothes-shop window, c. 1950

Henry Grant (born 1907)

Henry Grant was a freelance photographer who worked in London from the late 1940s until the early 1980s, together with his journalist wife, Rose. Much of their editorial work was for magazines and newspapers concerned with social or educational issues, such as the *Times Educational Supplement*. In 1986 the Museum bought the Grants' archive of prints and negatives.

Bill and Ben, the Flowerpot Men

Bill and Ben were two of the puppet stars of *Watch with Mother*, a children's television programme first screened in the 1950s. They came to the Museum in 1989 following the death of their creator Freda Lingstrom. The gift included other famous *Watch with Mother* puppet characters – Andy Pandy, Looby Loo, the Woodentops and Spotty Dog.

Latin American dance dress, 1955–65

This outfit was worn by a member of the famous Peggy Spencer formation dance team, based in Penge.

Mary Quant and Biba items, 1970s to 1980s

Mary Quant and Biba were two of the shops that helped create London's strong associations with youth fashion. Mary Quant's Bazaar opened in Chelsea in 1955, Biba opened in Kensington in 1964. In both cases cosmetics continued to be marketed after the closure of the original shops.

Packaging, 1960s to 1980s

The printed ephemera collection contains many types of packaging, including paper bags. The examples shown here come from some well-known London shops and a small sandwich bar in the City much used by taxi drivers.

THE WORKING HISTORY COLLECTIONS

London's economy underwent radical structural changes during the 1960s and 1970s. Many of the old-established manufacturing firms closed for good, others left London for other locations. The closure of the docks from the late 1960s symbolised the end of London's traditional economic character.

Curators responded to these changes by a systematic programme of recording London's disappearing trades and industries. The results strengthened the Museum's existing collection of working-history material by adding groups of tools, equipment and records from ninety-two London workshops and factories. Among the trades represented are ballet-shoe making, dyeing, glassmaking, clothing manufacture, boatbuilding, candlemaking, baking, buttonmaking and newspaper printing. Some of these workshop groups are now kept by the Museum in Docklands.

Suit, 1989

designed by Hardy Amies (born 1909)
The London fashion house of Hardy Amies was the subject of a recording project and exhibition in 1989. Museum staff recorded all the working activities of the firm, and acquired some of the firm's finished products, including this outfit (from the 1989 spring collection), which was donated by Sir Hardy Amies.

Printing plate for the front page of the *Guardian*, 1985

This printing plate was the last plate used by the *Guardian* when the newspaper was printed by the traditional hot-metal process. It is part of a group of material acquired to record a type of skilled work that disappeared rapidly with the development of new electronic printing processes.

A workman at Whitefriars glassworks, 1950s

When the Whitefriars glassworks closed in 1980 the Museum acquired its largest group of working-history material. The 8000 items included business archives dating back to the 18th century, tools, equipment, glass, paintings and photographs.

Port of London Authority policemen testing life jackets, 1930s

The Port of London Authority was established in 1909 to oversee the use and conservation of the River Thames. In 1973 it transferred its archive of records, artefacts and photographs to the Museum in support of the planned Museum in Docklands.

Badges, 1970s to 1990s
A selection of badges reflecting some recent London issues and campaigns.

Food packaging, 1993
The most important exhibition mounted by the Museum in recent years has been *The Peopling of London: 15,000 years of settlement from overseas*, which looked at the contributions made by overseas communities to London's unique character. These packages were all bought in London in 1993, as part of this project, to reflect the cultural diversity of the city today.

The Protein Man
From 1968 until 1993 Stanley Green could regularly be seen in Oxford Street campaigning against the dangers of eating protein, which he held responsible for the unwelcome social changes of the 20th century. When he died in 1993 the Museum acquired many items that belonged to him, including his placards and a complete set of his handprinted booklets *Eight Passion Proteins*.

Lubavitch Hasidic family, Stamford Hill, 1993 *(left)*
Magda Segal (born 1959)
This portrait of a London family comes from a series of photographs by Magda Segal, commissioned as part of *The Peopling of London* project. Her work gave the Museum a group of strong, sympathetic portraits of Londoners in their homes.

London Fields – The Ghetto, 1994 (detail) *(below left)*
James Mackinnon (born 1968) and Tom Hunter (born 1965)
The Ghetto is a model based on two streets in Hackney. Constructed from colour photographs and transparencies, it is nearly 6 metres (18ft) long and 3 metres (9ft) wide. It was made by a photographer, Tom Hunter, and an artist, James Mackinnon, inspired by the residents' campaign to save the streets from demolition.

The Enchanted Castle, 1990 *(right)*
Julian Perry (born 1960)
This is a bold and romantic vision of a Hackney Council tower block at Clapton Park. The Museum is an active collector of works by contemporary artists who are inspired and excited by their urban surroundings. Here, Julian Perry has animated what is usually seen as a drab urban landmark by a feeling of light, wind and vigour.

Spirit of Carnival, 1988

Tam Joseph (born 1947)

The Notting Hill Carnival is Europe's biggest street carnival and a symbol of the ethnic diversity of London today. For a brief period the carnival also came to symbolise the clash between authority and the spirit of cultural identity that carnival celebrated. This lithograph dramatises that clash.

Hat, 1993

designed by Philip Treacy (born 1947)

Made of stripped coq feathers for a photographic shoot for *Harper's Bazaar*, this hat displays the imaginative mastery of material and form that has made Philip Treacy one of Britain's foremost milliners. He gave it to the Museum in 1996.

THE ORAL HISTORY AND VIDEO COLLECTIONS

In 1992 the Museum established the post of Curator of Oral and Audio Visual History. The appointment recognised the importance of preserving individual Londoners' views, memories and life stories alongside the Museum's more traditional collections.

The oral history collection includes three groups of recorded material: tapes collected by the London History Workshop Centre in the 1980s, tapes made by the Museum in Docklands team as part of the working-history collections, and interviews recorded more recently by the Curator of Oral History and others. The latter are usually related to exhibition projects, such as *The Peopling of London*. The collection also includes video and film footage, plus a number of home movies shot by London families.

Mr and Mrs Martinez

Many interviews with members of London's ethnic communities were recorded as part of *The Peopling of London* project. Mr and Mrs Martinez recounted their impressions of London in the 1930s, when they arrived as refugees from the Spanish Civil War.

Servant girls, 1920s

These photographs show residents of a home run by the Metropolitan Association for Befriending Young Servants, a charitable organisation which offered accommodation and moral guidance to London's servant girls. The album was donated by Miss Louise Lenton after recording her memories of working for the association.

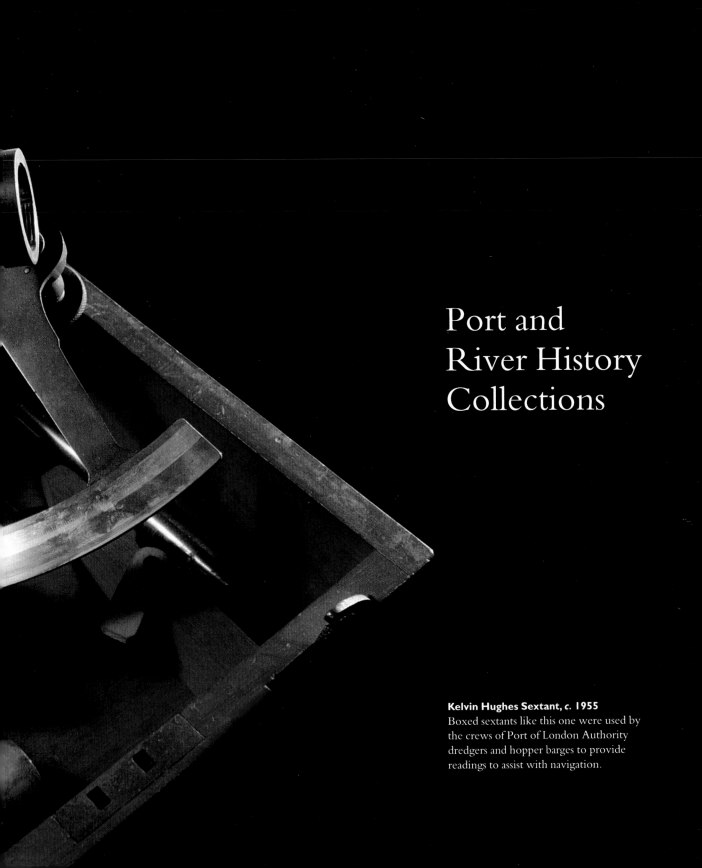

Port and
River History
Collections

Kelvin Hughes Sextant, c. 1955
Boxed sextants like this one were used by
the crews of Port of London Authority
dredgers and hopper barges to provide
readings to assist with navigation.

THE PROPOSED MUSEUM in Docklands will contain the rich collections acquired by the Museum of London over the past seventeen years. This unique programme of collecting and recording – along London's waterfront, in the historic port area and in the modern port area downriver – owes much to the support and encouragement of the London Docklands Development Corporation, the Port of London Authority, businesses and community organisations.

The new Museum has set its brief as River Port and People and will present and interpret the long and fascinating story of London as a world trading centre. The history of the Thames as a working river, which facilitated the transportation of people and goods, and gave rise to wharves, warehouses and the changing design of river vessels, is celebrated throughout this book. Indeed, without this important natural feature as its central artery, it is questionable whether London would have ever become a town, let alone a great metropolis and capital of the British Empire.

In the Museum of London, however, there is limited space and opportunity to display the rich and diverse collections which will be seen in the Museum in Docklands. On any scale, the range of the material is impressive. It includes the extensive historic and contemporary material which forms the Port of London Library & Archive, as well as Thames vessels, cargo-handling equipment, navigational items and models, together with port-associated processing and manufacturing trades. The list is almost endless, but contains boats, tugs, barges, cranes, winches, anchors, navigational buoys, vehicles, trucks, dock signs, models of ships and dock installations, commodity samples, occupational clothing, machinery and craftsmen's tools and equipment.

As a result of years of careful collecting and detailed research, it will be possible to recreate the complex story of the bustling trade, industry and community life which, for almost 2000 years, has made London one of the greatest international centres of the world.

Dock Sample Office, c. 1900
A detail from a recreation of a London dock sample office with just a handful of the many thousands of commodities which made their way to the 'Warehouse of the World'.

'W' Warehouse, Royal Victoria Dock
Some of the many thousands of port and Docklands artefacts added to the collections between 1979 and 1984, photographed in an impressive tobacco warehouse of 1883.

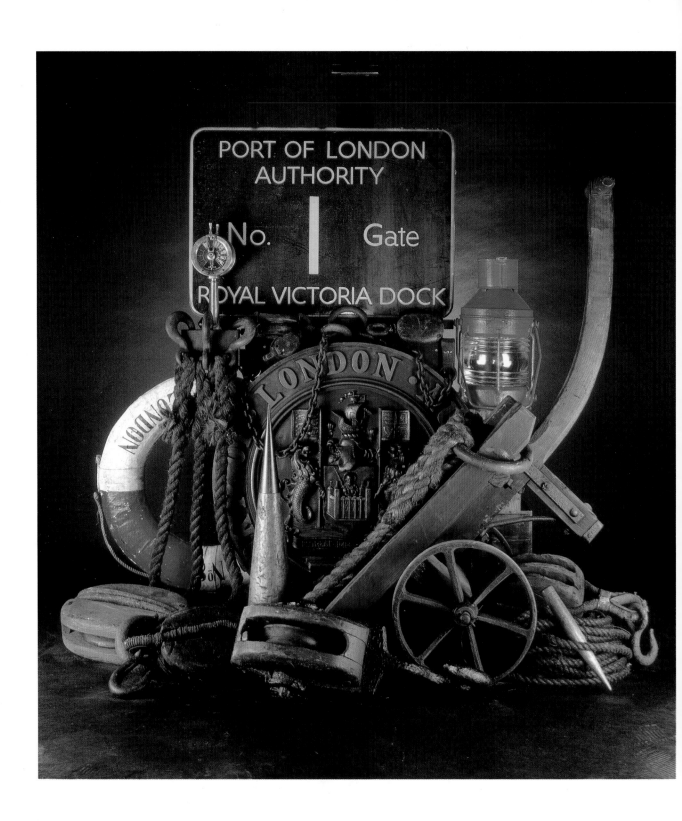

Group of dock items, c. 1870–1950 *(left)*
This group includes a bronze Port of London Authority coat of arms from a dock building, together with a lifebelt, ship's lamp, tea truck, cargo-sling, pulley-blocks and a rigger's set fid for working large diameter rope, and a dock gate sign.

Tobacco handling group, c. 1900–50 *(right)*
This reconstruction shows part of a tobacco weighing station from the Royal Victoria Dock. Tobacco was imported to London in vast quantities, in hogsheads, crates and bales. The large garbling knife was used to cut away any damaged tobacco from the imported lot. In the background is a typical warehouse Customs' cabin.

Dock cooperage, c. 1900–50 *(middle right)*
In this recreation of a typical dock cooperage can be seen all of the many tools and items of equipment which dock coopers used to maintain and repair barrels containing wines, spirits, sugar, tobacco, fruits, provisions, ginger, minerals and oils.

Rigger's workshop, c. 1900–50 *(below right)*
All the tools, equipment and products of the rigger can be seen in this reconstruction. For centuries, riggers have worked in the Port of London making and repairing both ships' rigging and cargo-handling gear.

Index